GOOD ETHICS
GOOD BUSINESS

GOOD ETHICS
GOOD BUSINESS
Your plan for success

Jacqueline Dunckel

Self-Counsel Press
(*a division of*)
International Self-Counsel Press Ltd.
Canada   U.S.A.

Printed in Canada

First edition: December, 1989

Canadian Cataloguing in Publication Data

    Dunckel, Jacqueline, 1930-
    Good ethics, good business

    (Self-counsel business series)
    ISBN 0-88908-857-8

    1. Business ethics. I. Title. II. Series.
HF5387.D86 1989174'.4C89-091410-9

*Trophy on front cover courtesy of Kelbert Trophies Ltd.,
1066 Richards Street, Vancouver, B.C., V6B 3E3*

Self-Counsel Press
(*a division of*)
International Self-Counsel Press Ltd.
Head and Editorial Office
1481 Charlotte Road
North Vancouver, British Columbia V7J 1H1

U.S. Address
1704 N. State Street
Bellingham, Washington 98225

CONTENTS

LIST OF WORKSHEETS

PREFACE

In undertaking to write this book, I interviewed educators, business people, and religious leaders. All agreed that in light of what was happening worldwide, scandal in government, business, religion, medicine, and sport, morals and ethics seemed to be something of the past. Blame was placed on a variety of causes. One man of the cloth quoted Fyodor Dostoyvsky's book, *The Brothers Karamazov:* "Without God, everything is permitted." Still another church leader sighted the breakdown of the family. A businessman blamed deregulation for the corrosion of ethics, while still another placed the fault on the "me generation." My media friends contended that the problems had always existed, but now, because of their efforts, people were being caught and exposed. One woman observed that "business ethics" was an oxymoron.

While their answers varied as to the crux of the problem, they all agreed with business guru Peter Drucker who has written that integrity is one of the few management qualities that cannot be learned or acquired; it must be brought to the job. Drucker feels that personal integrity is the basis for integrity in business.

The shock of having 100 of former U.S. President Reagan's officials facing allegations of questionable activities, of Canada's Prime Minister Mulroney's caucus colleagues being accused of unethical practices, of seeing white collar Wall Street wunderkind in handcuffs, and sport heroes stripped of their medals has caused owners, managers, and employees to examine themselves and their businesses. Business ethics has become the hottest subject on college and university campuses in North America with a 20% increase in student attendance over the decade. Even the games we play give an indication of our concern for the problem. *Trivial Pursuit* has been unseated by *Scruples*, a game in which players guess their opponents' responses to ethical dilemmas.

Whether ethics can be taught past puberty is not the question this book addresses. Nor do I attempt to place blame for the cause of the decline in business ethics. I have tried to present guidelines, not moral judgment. However, before we get into the guidelines, I want to share some of my findings, gleaned from books written for people who want to make their mark in the business world. I believe they suggest a climate which would foster greed and corruption. See if you agree.

- "The business world is boring, mundane, difficult, disgusting, humiliating."

- "It's a jungle out there. It's a rat race. You'll have little control over your destiny."

- "It's a long, slow road to success, so you had better find a shortcut. Switching jobs and loyalties is expected practice. Don't count on recognition, intelligence, and creativity — they aren't admired."

- "Don't trust anyone you work with. Never let down your guard."

- "Don't expect companies to have consciences."

- "There's no such thing as job security. Don't expect companies to be loyal to you."

- "Be ready to switch jobs with impunity and take your accounts with you."

- "Most companies do not use strategies outlined in *In Search of Excellence* because they take effort and time to administer."

- "The bottom line is the almighty dollar. They don't care how you make it, just make it."

If any of this has been your personal credo, or that of your company, don't expect change overnight. It takes from two to five years to move a company from unethical practice to ethical. Even then the process may be viewed with skepticism as merely a backlash reaction to headlines, a cosmetic approach to a blemish, or, even worse, a way to be perceived as ethical while still doing business as usual. Skeptics perceive the hiring of ethics consultants as a public relations answer to emergencies, not as a genuine step to change things. There seems to be some evidence to back this jaded thought. A Chicago business newspaper survey found that 99% of business respondents believed that "good ethics is good business," but 21% of the respondents stated they would slip a building inspector $100 if it would help speed things up. On the other hand, in 1988, 65% of Touche Ross directors felt that higher ethical standards makes a company a stronger competitor.

Are you now asking yourself "Why bother?" The answer is because the positives far outweigh the negatives. Companies that are unethical make the news; ethical companies do not. They just keep doing more business and make more profits. If you sincerely wish to improve your business ethics and those of your company...read on!

ACKNOWLEDGMENTS

With special thanks to Lisa Dunckel, H. Graham Donoghue, Julie Campbell, and Alsanne Wardrop.

1
ETHICS AND SMALL BUSINESS

As a small business person, you may feel that all the recent brouhaha over business ethics is just media hype and applicable to big business only. You may not have thought about how it relates to you or your business. Most of the news has centered on mega business and their lack of integrity and honesty. But most businesses began as "small" and grew. Some, like those founded by Rockefeller or by Ford, were based on an individual founder's code of ethics. Only when there was deviation from the code, or no code at all, did they flounder when they grew into big business.

It is true, there is nothing new about business ethics. Only the cynical would say that if you have one you cannot have the other. Ethics in business dates back before contracts and written agreements when a person's reputation was based on honesty and a person's word taken as truth. Recent history has focussed on honesty in every segment of society: politics, religion, culture, business — no one segment having a monopoly on truth. But honesty in business, unlike the other areas, can be measured in dollars: dollars legally or illegally obtained.

Unethical business practices have resulted in $200 billion lost annually to white collar crime while fines and penalties for law breaking add up to another $100 billion. When a company becomes news because of unethical practices, its good reputation is lost, and that cost can't be calculated. As North America becomes more and more a producer of services, the state of its employees becomes more of a concern.

It may be hard to measure morale in dollars, but when employees' pride plummets so does productivity and profits.

a. WHY RUN AN ETHICAL BUSINESS?

As a small business person, you set up your business to make money. You risked not only your investment dollars, but your reputation to start your business. What you can learn from history, both recent and past, is this: **If you want to be successful in business on a long-term basis, you must match your operational expertise with an ethical code of conduct practiced in every phase of your business.** No exceptions! Why? Because history has proven that ethical businesses succeed in the long run and, to put it bluntly, because business ethics can be measured in dollars. Sooner or later, unethical businesses get caught.

Now, let me hasten to say, that this does not mean that the incentive to operate an ethical business should be "so I don't get caught doing otherwise." Rather it is to set strong goals for continued growth and success.

Historically, small businesses, particularly small businesses in small towns, have enjoyed a reputation for operating honestly and ethically. Failure to do so has ruined owners. The satisfied customer has long been the foundation for small business success. Word travels quickly in a small center, particularly if it has to do with dishonesty, injustice, or scandal. While customer preference for many years was to larger chains and conglomerates, a more recent trend has been to smaller businesses. Customers want individual attention. They want to be able to talk directly to the person responsible for the service or product.

b. WHAT ARE BUSINESS ETHICS?

A short definition of ethics is "A system or code of morals and conduct of a person or group."

Philosophically, we can agree that the Mafia and marauding gangs have codes to which they strongly adhere. A strong code of behavior is demanded by certain religions and cultures as well. In some cases, these codes are both illegal in and abhorrent to our North American culture. On the other hand, people we admire and emulate have strong moral codes by which they govern their lives. I personally can name both my grandfathers, my parents, and several teachers or mentors as people who strongly influenced me because they conducted their lives based on personal codes of ethics.

Business ethics are based on the same kind of strong moral code. A business person plans for long-term success by operating an ethical business. Strictly adhering to the laws of the land, upholding the dignity of the profession, providing service to customers, being dedicated to quality, and showing loyalty to employees *along with* desiring to make a profit becomes part of the business code of ethics. The business person shows integrity by *always* adhering to that code.

c. YOUR COMMITMENT IS NECESSARY

Many small businesses are run by their owners, while others are run by managers hired by owners. Nearly all have one employee or more. All operate in a community, dependent on others for supplies and services. Management, employees, customers, and community are all involved in running an ethical business. Whoever is at the top, whether they are visible or invisible, must make the commitment and accept the challenge to operate an ethical business.

I reiterate: Once you have committed yourself and your business to a code of ethics, you cannot deviate from it. Nor can you have a code of ethics for your employees but not for yourself. *You* set the example. Whether you are an "on-the-scene owner" or an absentee owner, you must accept the responsibility of how your business is run.

3

This book examines the components of a business ethics program both from the owner's point of view and from the point of view of others. You, as a small business person, can gain a great deal of insight by looking at the situation from "the other side." Once your code of ethics has been set, you must follow those principles to set an example for everyone else. It all must come from the top: the initiative, the inspiration, the motivation, and the example.

d. ISN'T ABIDING BY THE LAW ENOUGH?

You may advance the theory that you are an honest, law-abiding citizen and that should constitute your basis for being an ethical business person operating an ethical business. But ethics goes further than that. Sound business ethics means a commitment to every factor of your business:

- to your customer or clients
- to the pricing, delivery, and servicing of your product or service
- to your employees
- to your suppliers or wholesalers
- to the maintenance of your work place
- to your community and environment
- to making a profit
- to becoming better

Johnson & Johnson is a very large, successful business with an excellent reputation. Notice how closely its credo adheres to the guidelines above:

> We believe that our first responsibility is to the doctors, nurses, hospitals, mothers and all others who use our products. Our products must always be of the highest quality. We must constantly strive to reduce the cost of these products. Our orders must be

promptly and accurately filled. Our dealers must make a fair profit.

Our second responsibility is to those who work with us — the men and women in our plants and offices. They must have a sense of security in their jobs. Wages must be fair and adequate and working conditions clean and orderly. Employees should have an organized system for suggestions and complaints. Supervisors and department heads must be qualified and fair-minded. There must be opportunity for advancement for those qualified and each person must be considered an individual standing on his own dignity and merit.

Our third responsibility is to our management. Our executives must be persons of talent, education, experience, and ability. They must be persons of common sense and full understanding.

Our fourth responsibility is to the communities in which we live. We must be a good citizen — support good works and charity, and bear our fair share of taxes. We must participate in the promotion of civic improvement, health, education, and good government, and acquaint the community with our activities.

Our fifth and last responsibility is to our stockholders. Business must make a sound profit. Reserves must be created, research be carried on, adventurous programs developed, and mistakes paid for. Adverse times must be provided for, adequate taxes paid, new machines purchased, new plants built, new products launched, and new sales plans developed. We must experiment with new ideas. When these things have been done, the stockholder should receive a fair return. We are determined with the help of God's grace to fulfill these obligations to the best of our ability.

As a small business person, you can make a similar commitment.

e. DOES RUNNING AN ETHICAL BUSINESS PAY OFF?

No writer of a book on business ethics is going to be able to give you great documents of proof that ethical businesses are more successful than those that aren't. Unethical businesses, caught in their dishonesty, make headlines. Other, very successful businesses, never make the six o'clock news. Whether or not they have a written code of ethics to follow, we may never know. But here are examples of two very diverse businesses that have set out to be ethical and the results are apparent.

One business sector that has had more then its share of scrutiny and scandal in recent years is the brokerage industry. One firm has managed to build itself into one of the top ten in the United States based on a credo of honesty. Chairman Chip Mason of Legg Mason in Baltimore, Maryland cites honesty, making a great deal of money for their customers, and not being greedy as their three basic principles of operation. The result of this policy?

(a) Since 1983 Legg Mason has annually increased its number of brokers by about 20%.

(b) Among 25 securities brokers (traded on all three major markets), the company has seen revenue growth that has been surpassed by only one other firm (Morgan Stanley).

But that's a big business success story, you say. What about a small business? While on vacation in Spain, I visited the beautiful city of Granada. One evening I decided to eat in the Plaza Mayor. Around the edges were many food vendors where you could buy your meal and take it to the tables set up in the plaza. I staked out a table and circled the booths, finally deciding on one furthest from my table. The booth was clean, the young man behind the counter helpful, the food appetizing. When the bill came, I put down my coins and returned to our table. Halfway through our meal, a frantic man approached me, his outstretched hand filled with coins. I had paid his son too much.

In our restricted bilingual conversation, he told me that his name was Enrique and that his father had started the business based on honesty and integrity. Now, he was passing this same standard on to his own son. The reputation of his business meant everything to him. He went to the market every day to choose the meat, the melons, and the wine himself. He bought only the best for his customers and they had come to expect only the best when they bought from him. I pointed out that I was a tourist and he could easily have kept the money. He pointed out to me that I might some day come back to Granada and he wanted me to be a "return customer." His business depended on satisfied customers and that was why he was still in his father's business while others had failed in the same location.

No matter where you are, the lesson is the same:

GOOD ETHICS = MORE BUSINESS = MORE PROFITS.

f. HOW TO USE THIS BOOK

This book is meant to help you develop your own ethics program. The following chapters examine the various issues that you must consider as you work toward implementation of your program. Three worksheets are included at the end of chapter 3 to help you do some preliminary assessment of yourself and your employees. (Answers are included in Appendix 3.) Once you know how you measure up, you can work out the nuts and bolts of your ethics plan. The final chapter, chapter 8, summarizes the topics you need to cover and gives you room to sketch out and write down your statements, assessments, and plans.

Finally, the appendixes give more food for thought. Appendix 1 provides examples of other businesses'codes of ethics; Appendix 2 poses some ethical dilemmas you can use for group discussion; Appendix 3 answers the worksheet questions from chapter 3, and Appendix 4 lists some references and resources you might find helpful.

2
WHAT SMALL BUSINESS CAN LEARN FROM BIG BUSINESS

Business ethics, or the lack of them, pushed religion, politics, and entertainment off the front pages in the late 1980s. While it certainly was not the first time that big business had come under close scrutiny, the modern media could expose more details more graphically than in the days of robber barons and Florida swamp land realtors.

Since the focus on business ethics, and probably your own basis for concern, stems from this recent attention to big business, we need to look at their experiences. There are lessons to be learned: both good and bad.

a. IMPLEMENTING A CREDO

While unethical behavior might appear to be expedient, common, and lucrative, companies that want to stay in business for the long term put quality of life for their employees and quality of service for their customers above short-term profit. Unethical companies put profit, at any price, first. Their biggest problem is greed.

Companies that stress business ethics usually have a written credo or mission statement to which they adhere. Johnson & Johnson's credo, for example (see section **d.** in chapter 1), addresses the need for business to make a sound profit while acknowledging the need to respect employees as individuals and to make high-quality products. This credo helped guide the company through its Tylenol tampering crises in 1982 and again in 1986 when seven people died after ingesting capsules containing cyanide. Officials at Johnson & Johnson kept clear heads and showed compassion and concern for public safety. They immediately set to work to tell the public that they would do everything to assure its safety. They recalled all of the products and set about designing tamper-free packaging.

We would be naive to believe that strong statements of ethics and good management assures that trouble won't happen. Boeing Aircraft has had a program of ethics firmly in place since 1964. Line managers lead training sessions, an ethics committee reports to the board, and a toll-free number is provided for employees to report violations. Despite this dedication, in 1984 a Boeing unit used inside information to gain a government contract. However, the reaction of the company was swift, and the employees responsible were fired. When a business has a policy in place, both management and employees know what is expected and what the consequences will be if the code is violated.

Xerox is another company that has been known to fire employees for violations of its code of ethics. Those violations were not necessarily a breach of the law, but a breach of a code that emphasizes integrity and concern for people. Xerox also places strong emphasis on hiring employees who share the same values as the company. It uses handbooks and guidelines for dealing with vendors, competitors, and customers. Periodically, it challenges its credos to see if they are still valid.

Imperial Oil, the Royal Bank of Canada, and Dow Chemical have also developed elaborate ethics programs that include codes of conduct, training workshops, ethics directors, company ombudsmen, and committees of management and directors that deal with moral issues. All of these companies agree that responsibility for ethics should not rest with the human resources or public relations departments, but must originate with the senior officers.

Evidence of trust and respect within the company is important to a company's image and reputation with the public. Because people trust Chrysler's Lee Iacocca, they believed him when he apologized for the company's unlawful practice of turning back odometers on executive cars before selling them to customers and assured them it wouldn't happen again. "We did it, we were dumb, it won't happen again," he said. This reassured the public. However, if such a thing does recur, it could destroy the public's trust in Chrysler *and* Iacocca for his name is synonymous with the company. He has become a father figure: the man who, many thought, might do for America what he did for Chrysler if he had chosen to run for President. We are not yet so jaded that we can shrug off being lied to by "father." Iacocca will have to maintain a comprehensive monitoring system to insure that all his employees and dealers act in an ethical, honest manner.

b. FOLLOW-THROUGH

Follow-through is very important in creating and maintaining an ethical business. In 1988, Earl Orser, president of London Life, advised every chief executive officer at this major brokerage house on new guidelines for its portfolio managers, traders, and other personnel — the people who invest about $400 million a day for London Life. Orser said the investment and trading employees must not deal personally with any institutional salesperson at any brokerage that is doing trades for London Life. All of these employees must make a monthly disclosure of their personal investments and brokers are urged to report any transgressions.

The success of such a program depends on follow-through. If there are transgressors, they need to be dealt with immediately and consistently. When a company has a code of ethics in place but does not adhere to it, then it is not worth the paper it's written on. Historically, the public had a great deal of trust in Henry Ford, his black motor cars, and his company. Most of us grew up believing that the Ford Motor Company's code of ethics was how the company did business. Their credo reads as follows:

AT FORD QUALITY IS JOB ONE

Mission

Ford Motor Company is a worldwide leader in automotive and automotive-related products and services as well as in newer industries such as aerospace, communications, and financial services. Our mission is to improve continually our products and services to meet our customers' needs, allowing us to prosper as a business, and to provide a reasonable return for our stockholders, the owners of our business.

Values

How we accomplish our mission is as important as the mission itself. Fundamental to success for the Company are these basic values:

People: Our people are the sources of our strength. They provide our corporate intelligence and determine our reputation and vitality. Involvement and teamwork are our core human values.

Products: Our products are the end result of our efforts, and they should be the best in serving customers worldwide. As our products are viewed, so are we viewed.

Profits: Profits are the ultimate measure of how efficiently we provide customers with the best products for their needs. Profits are required to survive and grow.

Guiding principles

Quality comes first: To achieve customer satisfaction, the quality of our products and services must be our number one priority.

Customers are the focus of everything we do: Our work must be done with our customers in mind, providing better products and services than our competition.

Continuous improvement is essential to our success: We must strive for excellence in everything we do: in our products, in their safety and value, and in our services, our human relations, our competitiveness, and our profitability.

Employee involvement is our way of life: We are a team. We must treat each other with trust and respect.

Dealers and suppliers are our partners: The company must maintain mutually beneficial relationships with dealers, suppliers, and our other business associates.

Integrity is never compromised: The conduct of our company worldwide must be pursued in a manner that is socially responsible and commands respect for its integrity and for its positive contributions to society. Our doors are open to men and women alike without discrimination and without regard to ethnic origin or personal beliefs.

Consumers lost faith when Ford dragged its feet on accepting the problems of its Pinto model in the 1970s. They felt the company had not acted in a socially responsible manner when Ford didn't react until court action prompted it to recall the cars in which several people died.

The lessons from big business are not just in how you deal with your customers, but also in how you treat your employees and your suppliers. Leona Helmsley, President of Helmsley Hotels, was accused in 1989 of evading federal taxes by diverting $4 million of business property to personal acquisitions.

What came out in the trial were tales of abuse and humiliation of her staff, compromising suppliers, and refusal to pay contractors for work completed and approved. When she refused to pay a meat supplier's bill of $8,500 because she disliked a corn beef sandwich and $353,191 to her renovator, they complained, first to the press, then to the grand jury. Suppliers also testified that she exhorted money, liquor, and television sets from them in order to get her hotel contracts. It was this testimony that proved damaging to Helmsley personally and to her company.

But instead of dwelling on the headline makers, let's look at two big businesses that set good examples and report consistently high profits. Lanier (Harris/3M) is a multi-national marketing, sales, and service company for copiers and facsimile equipment — a highly competitive industry. Lanier makes three basic guarantees to its customers:

(a) Ninety-eight percent guaranteed up-time or your money back for the time the equipment is down.

(b) A free loaner if your copier is out of service for more than eight hours.

(c) An after-hours, toll-free help line to assist you with minor emergencies.

This service has paid off. Lanier has enjoyed a 20% revenue growth rate in each of the past three years, 100% increase in facsimile sales over 1988, and product marketing arrangements with 102 countries.

The Chubb Corporation is another good example of a long-established company that is not just interested in "the bottom line." Back in 1882, Hendon Chubb stated, "While an insurance policy is a legal contract that expresses our minimum responsibility, there are many occasions when equity demands that we recognize a moral obligation beyond the strictly legal terms, and this is always a consideration in our settlements."

Today, the company's philosophy of looking past profits to people and community is stated in the company brochures: "The Chubb group has a very simple business philosophy. It believes in strict standards of business conduct and high standards of performance.

Chubb recognizes its responsibility to each of its clients as well as to its employees and its appointed agents and brokers. Chubb also recognizes its responsibility to society, as manifested by its matching gifts program, community outreach efforts, and vigorous support of public broadcasting."

Fortunately, this philosophy does not just appear on paper, but is the credo by which the company has governed itself for over 100 years.

c. THE LESSONS LEARNED

So what can you as a small person learn from these examples?

(a) If you set ethical standards for yourself, your company, and your employees, you all must live by them.

(b) You must have a way to monitor that they are being followed.

(c) You must have a means to retaliate if they are not adhered to.

(d) You must take the initiative to see they are followed, monitored and action taken if there is deviation.

(e) Most important, you, as the owner of the business (or your designate), must set the example. If you lose your reputation, you lose it all.

(f) Although you are in business to make money, if you make it at any price, by becoming greedy, you can be tempted to be unethical in your business practice.

3
DEVELOPING YOUR CODE OF ETHICS

a. WHERE TO BEGIN

Back in 1924, Edgar Heermance wrote *Codes of Ethics: A Handbook* in which he stated his belief that nothing is as powerful in reinforcing company and individual behavior as the written word: the company creed, philosophy, or code.

As the owner or manager of an ethical business, you set the standard for your employees. You must take time to formulate a code to see that it becomes reality. You must implement and monitor the credo, train personnel, and reward outstanding behavior. Not only do you carry the responsibility for increasing profits, but you also have a moral responsibility to your customers, employees, suppliers, and the environment. Former Bank of Montreal Chairman and C.E.O. William Mulholland has said, "Ethics in business is more than just a commitment not to lie, cheat, or steal. It is, or should be, a strong constructive and positive force in harmony with the values of the society which nurtures us. This is not just good citizenship, it is also good business."

If you are serious about wanting to own or manage an ethical business, you must approach the task not as though it is something cosmetic or transitory, but as a characteristic that will last the lifetime of your business. It must be a constant, practiced by everyone at every desk or counter, and over every telephone with every customer, employee, supplier, or other business contact. No exceptions can be made by anyone, particularly not by you the owner. It is you or your manager who establishes the norm and sets the standard.

If you only give lip service to business ethics, you cannot expect anything more from your employees. If you pad your expense account or arrange interest-free loans from the company, you should not be surprised when employees "borrow" pens and pencils from the office. If you do not set a high ethical standard, you should not be shocked if employees don't follow orders. You can't lecture staff on behavior while blatantly living a lifestyle that would stop the presses of supermarket tabloids. You can't demand that workers clock in and clock out on the dot if you're always late for meetings and "not available" on Friday afternoons. If you travel first class or take long lunch hours, you can't expect any great indication of economy, efficiency, and productivity from your staff. Don't expect employees to deal honestly with the company if company brochures don't tell the truth.

You must be accountable. If you misrepresent, exaggerate, or lie, you can expect your employees to do the same.

b. THE BASICS OF ETHICS

Business ethics must be based on pride, loyalty, integrity, honesty, and, on the part of management, leadership. Unless owners, managers, and employees have a mutual understanding of these basics, you cannot begin to establish your plan for good business ethics.

Before you start on your ethics plan, think about each of the following characteristics and how you define them.

1. Pride

Is pride the same as arrogance, conceit, or ego? Or do you think self-respect arising from accomplishment best describes pride? Pride in your work comes from a feeling of gratification as a result of associating with someone or something that is good and laudable. It is being and doing your best which gives you the right to be proud. Feeling proud about the work you do and the business you own or work for is the first step in setting a credo of ethics. You should be able to take pride in yourself, in the business and what it does, in work well done, and in your co-workers.

2. Loyalty

You may think of loyalty as a faithfulness to one's country, family, and friends, but you should also feel a certain loyalty to your business. Employees should also feel the same. It should not be blind loyalty, however, for you should question and approach problems with an open mind. Nor should loyalty in business be sentimental for sentiment can cloud judgment. Loyalty must be sincere; if you start with insincerity, you cannot begin to establish or maintain a plan for ethics in your business.

3. Integrity

Integrity is an unwavering adherence to one's principles. But people's moral principles can differ because of culture and environment. Someone who has very different morals from you may have a great deal of integrity and still conflict with your ethics plan precisely because he or she has integrity and stands by that other set of morals. To ensure that everyone in the company can demonstrate integrity in the company policies, you must be able to communicate with candor and sensitivity.

4. Honesty

Someone who is honest is truthful, free from deceit or fraud, law abiding, and incorruptible. A dishonest person will lie, cheat, steal, or otherwise break the law. Being honest is basic to establishing and maintaining a code of ethics. Dishonest acts on the part of managers or employees should not be tolerated and any reported act of dishonesty should be investigated. One dishonest employee can destroy the hard-earned good reputation of your business.

More important, if you fail to respond or overlook a dishonest act, you are implicitly approving it. Other employees, customers, suppliers, and the public will see it as the company's accepted way of doing business. Honesty in business means not only abiding by the laws of the land but being incorruptible in the face of temptation and not seeking to circumvent the law for expedience or gain.

Before you begin to consider putting together your plan, you must first look at yourself; your personal honesty, loyalty, and integrity will be the basis for your company's credo and reputation. Then you must look at the people who work for you. Everyone brings their own personal ethics with them. At the end of this chapter, you'll find a self-assessment test for you to work through (see Worksheet #1). Using this worksheet, you can rate yourself on a number of ethical management questions. A key to the worksheet can be found at the back of the book in Appendix 3.

c. GETTING THE RIGHT PEOPLE

1. Hiring a manager

If you are managing your business yourself, you can provide day-to-day leadership and act as a role model for your employees. If you hire someone else to manage your company, choose that person carefully, for he or she will be the model that others follow.

When hiring a manager, ask yourself the following questions:

(a) *How long have I known this person?* If your future manager has worked for you and come up through the ranks, you have had an opportunity to observe his or her performance, loyalty, honesty, and integrity. If you have hired from outside, you should investigate his or her background more fully and be prepared to monitor performance very closely.

(b) *Does my manager demonstrate the same concern, compassion, and interest in my employees that I do?* As a small business owner, you have come to realize that good business depends on attracting and holding good, dedicated employees.

(c) *Does my manager place the same value on quality products and service that I do?* You naturally want to see your profits build through good management, but you don't want your manager to sacrifice your reputation for quality and service in order to show an increase in profit.

(d) *Do my manager and I share basic beliefs of honesty and integrity?* If your manager thinks Oliver North was a great hero and you don't; if your manager boasts about how he or she cheated to get an MBA and you are shocked; if your manager finds the dilemma of an old woman trying to get across a street hilarious and you do not — you do not have a foundation for a strong business relationship. Here's a time when you need to respond to your gut feeling.

(e) *Is my manager's personal lifestyle an honest reflection of what I am paying him or her?* If you're driving a Ford and your manager or future manager drives a Porshe, your manager may be living beyond his or her means and may have to be "creative" to maintain that lifestyle.

2. Your other employees

In previous generations, it was not unusual for employees to remain with one company all their working lives. They were proud to have given years to "the railroad," "the school," "the store," or "the mine." In recent years, things have changed. Long-term employees may lose their jobs as part of a takeover or "downsizing" of their company while a "golden handshake" and forced early retirement may be the lot of other workers. Some small businesses sometimes find it cheaper to fire and rehire rather than increase wages for long-term employees. Therefore, today's employees may not develop any loyalty to their employers or their businesses.

If your business is to operate ethically, however, your employees must feel pride in the business and loyalty toward you. Employees bring codes of personal ethics to the job. They will have to make decisions based, in part, on those codes. You need to find the "straight arrow" employee who is honest, whose word can be trusted, and who has high principles. The winning formula is the ethical employee working for the ethical business. In a National Institute of Management poll, 72% of the 400 managers who responded said on occasion they had been disturbed by the unethical behavior of their supervisors. Another 37% reported they had to disregard their own personal codes of ethics in order to fulfill a task in their jobs.

New employees are affected by the actions of the other employees. Employees who steal, cut each other out of commissions, cheat clients, or take bribes or kickbacks set the example for others. You cannot afford to have one bad apple. If you tolerate any deviation from your code, you have no code.

When interviewing new employees, don't ask them what they *would* do in a possible situation; instead, have them tell you what they *did* do in an actual situation. Many companies are using this behavior identification interview technique to determine leadership and ethical qualities. At the end of this chapter, you will find Worksheet #2, which you can ask employees to complete in order to help you determine their basic ethics. A key to the worksheet is provided at the back of the book in Appendix 3.

Keep in mind that potential employees will also be rating you and your business based on your personal reputation, the reputation of the business with its employees, and the reputation of the company with its customers and suppliers. Ethical people want to work for ethical businesses to which they can make a commitment of loyalty, trust, and honesty.

d. THE IMPORTANCE OF LEADERSHIP

To build a business with honest employees who are proud of their work and who perform it with loyalty and integrity, you must demonstrate strong leadership abilities.

(a) *Reward excellence:* Expecting employees to do a job and do it well is not enough, and verbal appreciation with a pat on the back is just a beginning. Employee-of-the-month photos, recognition banquets, and bonuses are a few good ways to credit hard-working employees. Companies like Avon and Mary Kay give awards such as Cadillacs and diamonds; smaller companies find that tickets to football games or a weekend at a nearby resort can be well-received rewards. Be sure that competition for rewards does not breed animosity or dishonesty.

(b) *Allow and encourage employees to have input into business planning and goal-setting:* The employee who knows he or she has had an active role in solving problems and creating policies and procedures has a stake in the business and develops a strong sense of proprietorship and loyalty. A consignment clothing store in Calgary, Alberta called "Clothes Encounters" has two owners and two employees. They meet regularly to solve problems and work out the best way to reach its goals. All have an equal say and some of the best ideas have come from the employees.

(c) *Use a good performance review system:* A good performance review plan motivates people. It should include the following:

(i) Performance planning to set personal goals and objectives along with expected performance standards

(ii) Day-to-day coaching so managers and supervisors can help people accomplish their goals

(iii) Performance evaluation to evaluate performance against goals set

(iv) Adjustment, additional training, and modification of goals

A good performance review system allows an employee to grow, mature, and be more productive and to become a greater asset to the company. It is a strong evidence of good leadership. People don't mind working toward tough goals when they know their managers want them to succeed and will give them time and support. Companies that think that performance reviews are designed to find the worst in people will get employees who are also negative and who act selfishly and, on occasion, dishonestly.

(d) *Treat employees fairly:* During the 1989 takeover of Texaco Canada, Texaco employees cheered when they learned that Imperial Oil was the successful bidder. Imperial has a reputation for fair treatment of its employees. At least one of the competing bidders was harshly criticized as an uncaring employer who in a previous takeover stated that no employees would be terminated and two weeks later fired 150 people.

(e) *Clearly define your business goals:* It is essential to have a clear plan. You and your employees should have definite, agreed-upon goals and a time frame for achieving them. Don't be impatient and demand premature results, you may erode the self-esteem and loyalty of your employees and display erratic leadership qualities.

(f) *Listen to your staff:* You need good communication with your staff; giving orders does not constitute good communication. You need to listen to your staff, act on their good ideas, and reward them for helpful suggestions. This helps build self-esteem, pride, and loyalty.

(g) *Allow time for strategic planning, analyzing past and present business performance, and considering the pros and cons of a situation:* You need to allow staff members time to make decisions. Making a decision in haste may cost you more time plus money later on when you have to clean up the problems. Doing business takes time and thought to balance planning and implementation.

(h) *Follow these basic steps to find solutions to problems:*

  (i) Gather information from those involved and through your own observations.

  (ii) Get agreement on the right wording of the problem. This is not a superfluous task. If you cannot agree on the wording of a problem, you obviously understand it in very different ways. You must achieve consensus or you cannot begin to see a common solution.

  (iii) Give individuals time to reflect on the problem (10 minutes to half an hour).

  (iv) Exchange solutions as a group.

(i) *Define a policy regarding gifts:* Your policy might state that employees should not accept gifts from customers, suppliers, contractors, or anyone they work with outside the company. You might choose to bar gifts over a certain value, such as $5. Whatever your stance on this subject, it must be understood and obeyed by all staff members.

(j) *Obey all laws that pertain to your business:* Laws concerning safety, health, and protection of the environment must be monitored and enforced. If management doesn't comply with governmental regulations, employees will have no respect for the company's ethics. Government fines for polluting the air or water sources are very small when measured against profit. Unethical companies prefer to pay the small fines. Ethical companies will not only adhere to the regulations but go even further to assure they are well under the government guidelines. Staff members will obey company regulations only as well as the company obeys the laws of the land.

(k) *Pay your bills on time:* If you use suppliers as inexpensive bankers, you jeopardize your reputation. All commercial dealings need to be grounded in honesty, integrity, and respect for others if you are to win repeat business, which is the prerequisite for ongoing business.

(l) *Share the success of the company with your employees and the community:* Ethical companies are aware of corporate responsibility and try to be good corporate citizens. Big or small, they share their success with their employees and the community by giving employee bonuses and by sponsoring athletic and cultural events. The annual report of Hees International devotes five pages to its business values, which it summarizes as "fair sharing" of rewards among shareholders, clients, management, employees, and the community in relation to their respective contributions and the risks they assume. The owner of a smaller business can be equally responsible toward its employees and the community. The former publisher of *Canadian Hereford Digest*, Keith Gilmore, always shared the profits of the business with his eight employees through Christmas bonus checks. As one of those employees, I felt a sense of accomplishment for the part I had played in the magazine's success.

The size of the check was irrelevant: the commitment to staff was not.

If all of this sounds like what you would read in a personnel management manual, I can only reiterate that you must have this foundation before you can put together your code of ethics and the necessary procedures.

e. HOW DOES YOUR BUSINESS RATE?

Before beginning to implement a program of ethics, you must assess your present operation or, if planning a new business, consider the foundation requirements for an ethical business. Without pride, loyalty, integrity, honesty, and strong leadership in the company, any written code will remain merely meaningless words on paper. Worksheet #3 at the end of this chapter will help you rate yourself on your leadership capabilities. A key to the worksheet is provided at the back of the book in Appendix 3.

Circle the answer that best applies to you.

The basics

1. How do you rate your company in relation to others in the same field?

    (a) in the top 25%

    (b) in the top 50%

    (c) in the lower 50%

Ability

1. How do you rate your ability in your position relative to others in the same position?

    (a) in the top 25%

    (b) in the top 50%

    (c) in the lower 50%

Fostering pride

1. Do you sit down and discuss an employee's progress, problems, and activities?

    (a) regularly

    (b) sometimes

    (c) only when he or she needs reprimanding

2. Do you speak critically or run employees down to other employees?

    (a) never

    (b) rarely

    (c) frequently

3. Do you make a point of commenting on individual accomplishments?

    (a) always

    (b) sometimes

    (c) rarely

4. Do you criticize employees in front of others?

    (a) never

    (b) rarely

    (c) frequently

5. Would you make fun of an employee in front of others?

    (a) never

    (b) only when the other person does it to me

    (c) often, when joking

6. Do you point out when employees are wrong or correct them even though it serves no useful purpose?

    (a) never

    (b) frequently

    (c) rarely

7. Do you give recognition for a job well done?

    (a) always

    (b) sometimes

    (c) rarely

8. Do you direct and encourage your employees?

    (a) regularly

    (b) sometimes

    (c) never

9. Do you show enthusiasm for your employees' projects and efforts?

   (a) always

   (b) sometimes

   (c) rarely

10. Are you visible to your employees?

    (a) highly visible

    (b) occasionally visible

    (c) rarely visible

11. Do you demean an employee to make yourself look good in front of another employee or client?

    (a) never

    (b) rarely

    (c) often

12. Do you keep reprimands quiet and behind closed doors?

    (a) always

    (b) most of the time

    (c) sometimes

Building trust

1. Do you try to manipulate others by planning things to say to get them to act in a certain way?

   (a) never

   (b) sometimes

   (c) often

2. When disputes between employees arise, do you:

   (a) settle them immediately

   (b) take care of them when time permits

   (c) let them work themselves out

3. If you make a promise, do you follow through?

   (a) always

   (b) most of the time

   (c) sometimes

4. Do you go to bat for deserving employees?

   (a) always

   (b) most of the time

   (c) sometimes

5. Do you try to create group cohesiveness by sharing some unscheduled, informal, but not social time with employees?

   (a) always

   (b) most of the time

   (c) sometimes

6. If you make a mistake, do you own up to it in front of others?

   (a) always

   (b) most of the time

   (c) sometimes

7. Do you deal with performance problems at the first sign of trouble?

   (a) always

   (b) most of the time

   (c) sometimes

8. Do you give more chances to one employee than to another?

   (a) never

   (b) rarely

   (c) sometimes

9. Do you get rid of chronically poor performers?

   (a) always

   (b) most of the time

   (c) sometimes

10. Do you promise rewards that cannot be given?

    (a) never

    (b) rarely

    (c) sometimes

11. Do you praise a good worker for good work?

    (a) always

    (b) rarely

    (c) never

12. Do you reprimand a good worker for a mistake?

    (a) always

    (b) rarely

    (c) never

13. Do you ask employees to perform personal tasks for you?

    (a) never

    (b) rarely

    (c) often

14. Do you give performance and salary reviews on time?

    (a) always

    (b) most of the time

    (c) rarely

15. Do you stand by your word?

    (a) always

    (b) most of the time

    (c) as often as possible

16. Do you consistently treat every business associate and employee with respect and courtesy, regardless of their position?

    (a) always

    (b) most of the time

    (c) sometimes

17. Do you respect another person's property and space?

    (a) always

    (b) most of the time

    (c) sometimes

18. Do you respect a confidence?

    (a) always

    (b) most of the time

    (c) sometimes

19. Do you believe that gossip is harmless?

    (a) no

    (b) sometimes

    (c) yes

20. Do you return what you borrow?

    (a) always

    (b) most often

    (c) when I remember

Communications

1. You are not afraid to show your humorous side, but do not resort to humor that is in poor taste.

    (a) true

    (b) most of the time

    (c) false

2. You like to impress people with your knowledge and experience.

   (a) false

   (b) sometimes

   (c) true

3. Since you are the boss, it doesn't matter how well-groomed or well-dressed you are.

   (a) false

   (b) sometimes

   (c) true

4. When asked for help or information, you listen and respond sincerely without sarcasm or criticism.

   (a) always

   (b) most often

   (c) sometimes

5. You try to stimulate people to ask questions and express their ideas.

   (a) always

   (b) most of the time

   (c) sometimes

6. When talking to an employee, how much time do you spend listening?

   (a) more than 75%

   (b) 50% to 75%

   (c) 25% to 50%

7. Do you put off communicating about problems because you are uncertain of your ability to work out a solution satisfactory to the people involved?

   (a) never

   (b) sometimes

   (c) often

8. When talking to an employee, do you allow distractions (e.g., interruptions, telephone calls, etc.)?

   (a) never

   (b) sometimes

   (c) as they occur

9. Do you encourage people to express their viewpoints even if you do not agree with them?

   (a) always

   (b) sometimes

   (c) rarely

10. Do you interrupt others when you have an important point to make?

    (a) never

    (b) sometimes

    (c) often

11. Do you encourage a person to blow off steam, complain, or gripe?

    (a) in private

    (b) in a meeting

    (c) to others

12. Do you make sure that the persons involved are the first to know of an contemplated change and that the information comes directly from you?

    (a) always

    (b) usually

    (c) rarely

13. When information is important, do you inform in writing and then reinforce verbally (or vice versa)?

    (a) always

    (b) sometimes

    (c) rarely

14. When you have an important change to communicate, do you welcome discussion of reactions, get feedback, and follow up?

    (a) always

    (b) sometimes

    (c) rarely

15. If policies, rules, and objectives are important, do you make sure that those involved are completely aware of them?

    (a) always

    (b) sometimes

    (c) as often as possible

16. Do you respect other's feelings and opinions?

    (a) always

    (b) sometimes

    (c) not usually

Honesty

1. Would you whitewash a poor worker's performance evaluation in order to keep the peace?

   (a) yes

   (b) no

2. Do you have a good performance review system in place with set goals and objectives and always evaluate performances against these goals?

   (a) yes

   (b) no

3. When you hire new employees, do you tell them that the company will not tolerate dishonesty? If there is positive evidence of their dishonesty, do you fire them?

   (a) yes

   (b) no

4. Do you send employees to training sessions without telling them why they are being sent?

   (a) yes

   (b) no

5. Do you use training courses to evaluate an employee's performance?

   (a) yes

   (b) no

6. Do you rate your supervisors by the way they rate their staff?

   (a) yes

   (b) no

7. If a good customer wrongfully placed the blame on one of your employees and demanded you reprimand the employee, would you do so?

    (a) yes

    (b) no

8. Do you compromise or bypass a previously agreed decision-making process in order to get quick results?

    (a) yes

    (b) no

9. Would you compromise the standards of your product or service to get a large contract?

    (a) yes

    (b) no

10. Do you demand results, at any cost?

    (a) yes

    (b) no

11. Would you choose "not to see" when an employee is receiving gifts from a supplier who is giving the company a good deal even though you have a company policy against employees receiving gifts?

    (a) yes

    (b) no

12. Would you continue to do business with a supplier who offers kickbacks to you or an employee?

    (a) yes

    (b) no

13. When answering any of these questions, did you look ahead at the key at the back of the book so you would give the "right" answer?

    (a) yes

    (b) no

WORKSHEET #2
EMPLOYEES AND ETHICAL ISSUES

Circle the answer that best applies to you.

Pride and ability

1. How do you rate this company in relationship to others in the same field?

    (a) in the top 25%

    (b) in the top 50%

    (c) in the lower 50%

2. How do you rate your ability in your field in relationship to others?

    (a) in the top 25%

    (b) in the top 50%

    (c) in the lower 50%

Fostering self-esteem in others

1. Do you sit down and discuss your work problems with your supervisor or employer?

    (a) regularly

    (b) sometimes

    (c) only when I feel I'm about to be reprimanded

2. Do you criticize or run down other people when talking to other employees?

    (a) never

    (b) rarely

    (c) occasionally

3. Do you criticize or gossip about your boss behind his or her back?

    (a) never

    (b) rarely

    (c) occasionally

4. Do you make a point of congratulating a co-worker when he or she does something well?

    (a) often

    (b) occasionally

    (c) never

5. Do you make a point of telling your boss that he or she has done something well?

    (a) often

    (b) occasionally

    (c) never

6. Do you criticize co-workers in front of others?

    (a) never

    (b) rarely

    (c) sometimes

7. Do you make fun of co-workers in front of others?

    (a) never

    (b) only when the other person does it to me

    (c) often, when I'm joking

8. Do you show enthusiasm for your boss's projects?

    (a) often

    (b) rarely

    (c) never

9. Do you encourage other employees in their work?

    (a) often

    (b) occasionally

    (c) never

Trust

1. Would you knowingly act in an unethical way?

    (a) never

    (b) in order to retain my job

    (c) if I could make more money

2. When disputes occur between other employees, what do you do?

    (a) speak up if someone is being treated unfairly

    (b) stay out of it

    (c) take sides

3. If you make promises, do you follow through?

    (a) always

    (b) most of the time

    (c) sometimes

4. If you make a mistake, do you own up to it in front of others?

   (a) always

   (b) most of the time

   (c) sometimes

5. If you discovered a co-worker doing something unethical, what would you do?

   (a) speak to that person first about it

   (b) report it to the boss first

   (c) say nothing

6. Do you ask co-workers to cover for you?

   (a) never

   (b) rarely

   (c) sometimes

7. Do you stand by your word?

   (a) always

   (b) most of the time

   (c) as often as possible

8. Do you treat your employer, co-workers, and suppliers with the same respect and courtesy regardless of their position?

   (a) always

   (b) most of the time

   (c) sometimes

9. Do you respect another person's property and space?

    (a) always

    (b) most of the time

    (c) sometimes

10. If someone gives you information in confidence, do you respect that confidence?

    (a) always

    (b) most of the time

    (c) sometimes

11. Do you believe gossip is harmless?

    (a) yes

    (b) sometimes

    (c) no

12. If you borrow something, do you return it?

    (a) always

    (b) most often

    (c) when I remember

13. If you felt your boss was acting as judge and jury about your performance would you:

    (a) discuss it rationally

    (b) ignore it

    (c) get even

Communications

1. You are not afraid to show your humorous side, but do not resort to humor that is in poor taste.

   (a) true

   (b) most of the time

   (c) false

2. You like to impress others with your knowledge and experience.

   (a) false

   (b) sometimes

   (c) true

3. If you work out of sight of clients or customers, it doesn't matter how well groomed you are.

   (a) false

   (b) sometimes

   (c) true

4. When asked for help or information, do you listen and respond sincerely, without sarcasm or criticism?

   (a) always

   (b) most of the time

   (c) sometimes

5. When talking to your boss, how much time do you spend listening?

   (a) more than 75%

   (b) 50% to 75%

   (c) 25% to 50%

6. When talking to your co-workers, how much time do you spend listening?

    (a) more than 75%

    (b) 50% to 75%

    (c) 25% to 50%

7. When talking to clients or customers, how much time do you spend listening?

    (a) more than 75%

    (b) 50% to 75%

    (c) 25% to 50%

8. When talking to fellow employees you:

    (a) encourage and share information

    (b) gripe

    (c) gossip

9. When you don't understand an order, a memo, or directive you:

    (a) ask for clarification

    (b) follow what someone else is doing

    (c) ignore it

10. When information is important, do you inform in writing and then reinforce verbally (or vice versa)?

    (a) always

    (b) sometimes

    (c) rarely

11. When an important change is announced by your boss or supervisor, you:

    (a) accept without question

    (b) make sure you understand it before you accept it

    (c) oppose it on the basis that change usually means more work

12. Do you consider yourself open and honest in your communications, but still respect others' feelings and opinions?

    (a) yes

    (b) no

Honesty

1. Do you feel that business supplies are free for the taking?

    (a) yes

    (b) no

2. Do you welcome your performance review?

    (a) yes

    (b) no

3. In all your working relationships (i.e., with employer, employees, clients, customers, suppliers, etc.), do you let it be known that you will not tolerate dishonesty?

    (a) yes

    (b) no

4. If you were asked to cut corners in quality in order to increase profit, what would you do?

5. If a supplier offered you a kickback, what would you do?

6. If your boss was doing something illegal, would you report him or her?

    (a) yes

    (b) no

WORKSHEET #3
RATING YOUR LEADERSHIP QUALITIES

Choose the sentence that best describes you.

1. (a) I am the person people often turn to for direction.

   (b) I look after my own interests first.

2. (a) Because I am honest myself, I can be ruthless if others are not.

   (b) I intend to survive and will create my own rules if necessary.

3. (a) I enjoy consulting on complex issues and problems.

   (b) I enjoy planning, directing, and controlling my staff to ensure the highest profit margins.

4. (a) I enjoy playing team sports, even doubles in tennis over singles. I particularly like to captain the team.

   (b) I choose single sport activities where I compete against myself or one other person.

5. (a) I usually give people the benefit of the doubt, rather than engage in an argument.

   (b) I enjoy confrontation.

6. (a) I stick to a problem even when I am getting nowhere.

   (b) If I cannot solve a problem quickly, I become bored and drop it.

7. (a) I take responsibility for how well others do their work.

   (b) Whatever I do, I have to do it better than anyone else.

8. (a) I praise others and give credit when it's due.

   (b) I like people, but have little confidence in their abilities to do things correctly.

9. (a) I like to deal with people on a personal level.

   (b) I like to work where money and profits are more important than employees' well-being.

10. (a) I am willing to take the advice of others even though it may mean changing company plans.

   (b) Once I have set a goal, the goal becomes all important.

4
GETTING IT DOWN ON PAPER

The exercises in the previous chapter allowed you to evaluate yourself, your employees, and your way of doing business. You can now proceed and begin working on putting your code of ethics on paper if —

(a) You are totally committed to having an ethics program

(b) You take the time to write a mission statement first

(c) You allow time for you and your employees to write a code of ethics

(d) You are adequately financed and prepared to spend money to develop the program, communicate it to your employees, train employees, and implement the program. It costs money in the short term to be ethical in the long term.

Continue to read the following chapters and applying the principles to your business. When you are ready, use the lists and questions in chapter 8 to put your plan together.

a. OWNER/MANAGEMENT RESPONSIBILITY

You must always remember that codes of ethics are not just for employees to follow. Andrew Sigler, Chairman of Champion International, said that it was the corporate credo that helped guide the company through its 1988 reconstruction. The problem at that time of meeting budget restraints came down to laying people off or honoring the company's commitment to its employees. In the end, no one was fired because the company cut expenditures in other areas. Management stuck by its credo.

Your commitment to your business's credo is critical to its success. Having a written ethics code means nothing unless you follow it. An example of this is the Los Angeles-based defense contractor who was a participant in the Defense Industry Initiatives on Business Ethics and Conduct and who was accused by employees of overcharging the government more than $2 billion dollars on the Stealth Bomber program. A code was in place, but it was proved worthless by the deceit of putting a frame around the code but never reading or heeding it again.

In contrast, when Timothy Eaton of the Eaton's Department Store chain in Canada said to his employees in 1869 that they were never to use any deception in even the smallest degree — "nothing you cannot defend before God and man" — he set himself as an example to his staff and held himself responsible for their well-being and his own actions.

b. THREE RULES FOR OWNER/MANAGERS

(a) Determine your own accountability and responsibility. Accept them as essential to ethical management.

(b) Take responsibility for what is going on in your business. Any time you don't know about unethical behavior, your business is in trouble.

(c) Take responsibility for what happens within the company.

Two recent cases where management did not follow these three rules were the Iran-Contra Affair and the over-drafting practices of E.F. Hutton, Incorporated. In both cases, the people at the top exonerated themselves because they believed what they were told by staff or they preferred not to listen.

It is sobering to think that the president and the board of one of the country's largest investment firms didn't know its employees were acting contrary to the law, but even more sobering when neither the president nor the vice president of the country knew that "an employee" was selling arms to Iran and diverting the money to the Nicaraguan Contras in defiance of Congress.

E.F. Hutton was a reputable 83-year-old company that had huge success in the 1970s but no long-range strategic planning for the 1980s; it squandered millions on questionable expense accounts. Greed resulted in 2,000 counts of fraud. No Hutton executive was indicted, but the company's good name was tainted. Not even hiring Bill Cosby, one of television's most credible performers, to act as a spokesperson could save them. Finally, the company was auctioned off in 1987 to Shearson Leahman Brothers.

c. WRITING A MISSION STATEMENT

Whether you are just starting a new business, already running one, or taking over an existing business or franchise, you need to have a mission: a reason for being in business. To make money is a good reason, but it is a very narrow objective. Making money can be done in many ways. If you are committed to making money honestly and with a moral conscience, your mission needs to be expanded and written out so anyone doing business with you can read it.

A mission statement sets out, usually in one sentence, why your company is in business and how it intends to do business. A mission statement is an accurate and meaningful statement of your company's goals, objectives, and purposes.

When writing your mission statement, consider the following questions:

(a) Why are we in business?

(b) What does this business want to achieve?

(c) What methods will we use to make our achievements?

(d) Who is involved in making these achievements?

(e) Who will buy our service or product?

(f) Where will we conduct our business?

(g) When will we conduct our business?

Eddie Bauer of Expedition Outfitter, a company headquartered in Seattle, displays its mission statement in every store:

> This is our creed:
>
> To give you such outstanding quality, service, and guarantee that we may be worthy of your highest esteem.
>
> This is our guarantee:
>
> Every item we sell will give complete satisfaction or you may return it for a full refund.

Yes, it goes beyond one sentence but it clearly states why they are in business and how they will go about doing business.

Once you have your mission statement written, you must look at it as the "motto" by which your business will grow and prosper.

d. DEVELOPING YOUR CODE OF ETHICS

Your next task is to develop your code of ethics; it backs up the mission statement and sets the standard of behavior required to fulfill the mission statement. A code of ethics might be simply stated. McDonnell Douglas, an aircraft manufacturer, has a corporate ethics policy that simply states that employees should be "honest and trustworthy in all relationships."

Your code of ethics may be just as simple or more explicit and all-encompassing. Some large companies have book-size codes that cover every aspect of behavior.

A code of ethics might state that no employee will undertake any activity while on company premises or engage in company business that is or gives the appearance of being illegal or immoral or that could harm or embarrass the company or the customers. It can also cover conflicts of interest, proprietary information, political contributions, activities outside the company, improper transactions and payments, anti-trust compliance, community relations, treatment of company property, obligation to shareholders, working conditions, basis of promotions, equal opportunity, roles of internal and independent auditors, boards of directors, safety, the media, and suppliers.

You may find all of that overwhelming, but it needn't be if you get down to basics. As a small business person, you operate a business that sells either a product or a service to a client or customer. You buy your materials from one or more suppliers. You employ personnel to assemble the product or design the service and sell it. Other employees may service the product. Your business is governed by certain laws and regulations. There are business taxes, insurance, and permits to be paid. You may have borrowed money. There may be stockholders or silent partners or backers. You may advertise your service or products. Every one of these aspects of business has far-reaching legal and moral ramifications and should be considered when writing your code of ethics.

Your code of ethics should not be a "dictum" from on high. You need to involve yourself, your staff, and your silent partners or backers if you have them. Your staff will have a greater sense of commitment if they are also the architects of the plan. Your silent partners or your backers should share your vision of your business and be committed to it. Their moral and ethical reputation is as important to the business as yours.

You should also beware of putting together your code in haste. Set aside time for discussion and, if possible, retreat to a neutral location so you can concentrate without distractions. You may wish to use an outside resource person who will keep discussions on track and nurture the process, who can point out the discrepancies between myth and fact, and who can help steer discussion through the gray areas that can cause ethical dilemmas.

e. SOME OF THE QUESTIONS YOUR CODE SHOULD ANSWER

When you sit down to develop your business code of ethics, be sure to address these questions:

(a) What are your basic concerns (honesty, integrity, loyalty, obeying the law, respect for property, respect for others)?

(b) Who must comply (staff, management)?

(c) Who will be affected (customers, suppliers, the other companies, the media, the environment)?

(d) Where must compliance take place (on site, off site, customer locations)?

(e) When do you expect compliance? (during working hours, at all times)?

(f) Why is the code needed (to protect whom, offer service to whom, assure quality, service)?

(g) Why is compliance expected (so that there can be ongoing trust, quality, service, loyalty, etc.)?

(h) What kind of compliance is expected (immediate, without question, with careful consideration of the pros and cons, using guidelines provided, with help from others)?

(i) How can employees determine if it is the right decision (is it fair and balanced, are they comfortable with the decision and would they be pleased to see it on the front page of the newspaper)?

(j) What are the consequences of ignoring the code (reprimands, fines, firing)?

(k) Who will be responsible for judging the nonaction or action contrary to the code (ombudsman, ethics committee)?

(l) How will the success of the code be monitored and evaluated and by whom?

(m) What is the decision-making structure? Does it allow for future change?

5
YOUR PRODUCT OR SERVICE

So far, I have emphasized the "people part" of putting together your code of ethics, and I address that area more specifically in chapter 6. But you must also include your product or service when you think about your code. You may be a committed, loyal owner with equally committed, loyal employees, but if you are not producing an ethically made product or providing sound service, yours is not an ethical business. Furthermore, if you are not ethical in advertising your product or service, you compound the problem.

a. PRODUCT

If your business produces a product, your code of ethics should include all of the following (or more):

(a) The standard by which the product is produced

(b) The quality of the materials used to produce the product

(c) Under what conditions the product is produced

(d) Whether the product is exclusive

(e) What the product will do

(f) Whether you guarantee the product (how and for how long)

(g) How the product will be serviced (if applicable)

(h) Who will do the servicing

(i) How the product is priced

(j) How you compete with similar products

(k) What you do if the product is unavailable

McDonald's, Wendy's, and Burger King emphasize the quality of the ingredients that go into their hamburgers. They guarantee their customers that each burger will be a certain weight and will be fresh. Levi's stresses the quality of materials and guarantees the work in their jeans. If you have stated in your mission statement that you produce quality widgets, for example, your code of ethics should include every step that determines that quality. If your mission statement declares you will stand by that product, your code of ethics must clearly state what you mean by "stand by" as far as guarantees and services are concerned.

You may not produce the products yourself; you may buy then from wholesalers. Your code of ethics should state what your standards are for selecting that merchandise and your criteria concerning materials and quality. In this day of counterfeit Gucci watches and rip-off Lacoste shirts, you need to be specific about the type of merchandise you sell. Even highly touted name brand items, particularly clothing, can be poorly manufactured. Your code needs to state clearly how you select all your merchandise.

b. SERVICE

Plumbers, electricians, seminar leaders, lawyers, and chiropractors provide a service to their clients or customers. If yours is a service business, you should include some, all, or more of the following information in your code of ethics:

(a) What your standard of service is

(b) How it will be delivered (condition, place)

(c) When it will be delivered (8:00 a.m. to 4:00 p.m., 24 hours)

(d) Who will deliver it (the training, decorum of the staff)

(e) Quality of materials used

(f) Service guarantees

Many businesses offer both products and service. If yours is one of those, your code must reflect both aspects. For example, Domino's Pizza guarantees delivery (the service) of their pizza (the product) within a certain time or the customer gets the order free.

c. ADVERTISING ETHICS

I was in a supermarket in Denver recently when a man threw a package of bologna at a cashier and made his way out loudly berating the store's advertising practices. The cashier simply sighed and said "Oh, this happens every time we run an ad." Unethical advertising? When I checked the counter where the special was displayed, I found a prominent sign advertising the brand on special under which were many packages of bologna, some at a special price and some not. I had to sort through to find the bargain bologna; the regularly priced bologna far outnumbered those specially priced.

Advertising ethics is another area you should address in your code. I was delighted when Andy Rooney on "60 Minutes" took the airlines to task regarding their advertising of low fares. While it was true that low fares were being offered, consumers had to read the small print to find out the limitations: it was necessary to book months ahead and travel on specified days and during off-hours. The advertising was technically honest, but most people would consider it unethical because it wasn't up front.

Several years ago, advertisers were exposed for filming soup with marbles in the bottom of the bowls to make the soup appear as though it were brimming with meat and vegetables. In other cases, red dye was added to give the appearance of ripeness on some vegetables and greens were sprayed with sulfites to appear fresh.

New rules and regulations regarding advertising are now in effect, but your code of ethics should spell out clearly how your business promotes itself.

1. Product advertising

First and foremost, the product advertised should be the product sold. Any pictures or descriptions of your products must be accurate. For example, if your advertising talks of product freshness, make sure you can back it up. John Hughes became chief executive office of Fanny May Candy Shops in 1981. Since that time the company's share of the $12 billion-a-year retail candy market has increased 90%. One of Hughes' guarantees to his customers is freshness, which is backed by dating the product and pulling the candy from the shelves on a rigidly adhered to schedule.

All "sales" should be genuine; prices must be marked down from the original. Ensure that there is sufficient inventory, and don't try to substitute another product when you run out. Instead, offer rain checks if you run out of the product before a sale closes. Don't include any exceptions to the terms of sale in the fine print of an advertisement that many consumers won't read.

2. Service advertising

If you advertise a service, you must deliver what you promise. If you guarantee your service, you must spell out the guarantee and how it will be supported. I once employed Reggin Roofing Contractors of Calgary to tar a flat top roof for me. They would not take my check until after it had rained so I could be certain the roof wouldn't leak. That guarantee was part of their advertised service and they followed through on it.

Your code of ethics should address the following points regarding your service advertising:

(a) What your service includes — there should be no hidden costs

(b) What the guarantee is on the service — if there is a time factor it should be included in large print

(c) What the qualifications are of the people providing the service

(d) How the service will be delivered

(e) When it will be delivered

(f) When the service is available — toll-free help lines are great additions to service but must be maintained at all times by competent personnel.

6
YOUR CODE OF ETHICS AND THE PEOPLE AROUND YOU

a. YOUR BUSINESS AS A PARTNERSHIP

How encompassing you wish your code of ethics to be is entirely up to you. But let me put forth the theory that your business is a partnership with:

- Your backers or silent partners
- Your franchiser
- Your bank
- Your lawyer
- Your auditor
- Your insurance agent
- Your suppliers
- Your employees
- Your customers

How successful your business becomes depends largely on these partnerships. Ethical behavior must be practiced by everyone involved. Some partners you cannot monitor, but others you can and, therefore, you must decide if you want to include these partners in your code of ethics. When choosing your backers, banker, lawyer, auditor, or insurance agent, you should ask these questions:

(a) What is the reputation of the firm internationally, nationally, and locally?

(b) What is the business reputation of the person I am doing my company business with?

(c) What is the personal reputation of the person I am doing business with?

(d) How long has the firm been in business?

(e) What is the business track record of the person I am doing my company business with?

(f) How long has that person been with this firm?

(g) Has the firm said or done anything that makes you question how they would represent you or your business?

(h) Have they suggested any procedures that could be construed as dishonest, immoral, or unethical?

(i) Do your "partners" trust you? Have you given them any reason to question your ethics?

As a small business person, you need to choose your "partners" very carefully. Backers may put pressure on you to make a bigger profits faster, at whatever cost. Banks may be eager to give you a loan initially but have a reputation for pulling out the support at the time of renewal. You also need solid evidence and unquestionable adherence to the law from your lawyer, bookkeeper, and auditor. How they advise and represent you can have positive or negative results on your business.

You may wish to include in your code of ethics some guidelines for choosing some of these partners. If you already have most of your partners in place, it isn't too late to run an ethics check. You can always make changes.

I suggest you build all partnership relationships very slowly. You may act as if you trust, but don't. Question. Evaluate. Always stay informed about your partners:

- How are they acting on your behalf?

- Has the relationship changed in any way?

- Has the firm undergone any changes that will ultimately affect you?

If new people have been assigned to do business with you, don't accept the change without question. Redo your ethics check. Previously ethical businesses can become unethical because of greed and/or pressure put on the owner/manager from one or more of their own partners.

b. THE SENIOR PARTNERS

The "senior partners" in your partnership are your employees, your customers, and your suppliers.

1. Your employees

In chapter 3, I discussed the importance of hiring good people — people who shared your perception of moral and ethical behavior. In putting together your code of ethics, you now have to look at the issue from both sides: yours and your employees.

(a) Developing an ethical attitude in your employees

You need to sit down with your employees and discuss expectations: both yours and theirs. You all need to be clear on what you consider appropriate and ethical behavior. Consider these questions:

- What behavior of conduct do you expect from employees?

- What behavior of conduct can they expect from you and the business?

- What is expected from the employee if that behavior is breached or compromised?

- What is expected from you if that behavior is breached or compromised?

- Does your business have problems in systems that could cause employees to make unethical decisions? If so how can they be corrected? Can you develop guidelines that they can follow when the problems arise?

- Are your employees working in an ethical environment? What can you put in your code that will guarantee that they will not juggle the books, compromise product or services, or otherwise be compromised?

- Do you want to include compensation, rewards, promotions, benefits, and safety in your code of ethics?

- Do you want to include in the code the extent that employees are involved in business decisions?

As already mentioned, each individual brings his or her personal set of ethics to work. Graduate engineers, for example, have a professional code of ethics. As an employer, you should insist that your business's code of ethics helps build and support strong personal and professional ethics that are based on pride, self-esteem, trust, and commitment. It should encourage pride in self, in work, and in the company. (An unhappy, disgruntled, or frustrated employee is vulnerable to unethical behavior. If you have an employee whose attitude has changed, who is dumping work on others, falsifying or stealing, calling in sick, you need to deal with the problem immediately and in a straightforward manner.)

No employee should ever feel the need to cover up, lie, or exaggerate in order to please an employer. Your business code should allow reward for accomplishments to build employee self-system. Trust is mutual. Your business code should emphasize the trust in which the company holds the employee. As the owner/manager, your input into writing the code should emphasize the commitment to the employee. Then you must assure that you stand by the commitment.

Your code should also include the commitment of employee to the business, the product, or service. (An employee who is unhappy with the money he or she is making, who will not be more productive, or who does not have a strong commitment to the product or service, should seek counselling either within the company or outside or resign.) Employment is an agreement between employee and employer. Many small businesses fail either because the employer does not live up to his or her agreement with employees or because employees demand more pay than the business can afford. Caught between the demand for more money from financiers and more pay from employees you may find yourself compromising your ethics. I can only caution you again to choose your partners carefully.

(b) Guidelines for decision making

A code of business ethics should spell out what behavior is expected of you, your business, and your employees but be sure it also includes guidelines to follow when confronted with an ethical problem. Here are some basic questions you and your employees can ask yourselves about a decision or action. You and they may add to them when drawing up your code of ethics and the procedures to follow:

(a) Is it legal? Obeying the laws of the land is primary. If it is not legal, don't do it!

(b) Does it conform to the company's code of ethics and standards? It may not be illegal, but if it doesn't conform to your code of ethics, don't do it. If you are unsure, get a second or third opinion before you proceed.

(c) Is it balanced or fair? Will the decision be fair to all concerned or will one party benefit more over another in the short or long term? If the decision benefits one side at the expense of another, it can create animosity and resentment. Weigh the effects of your decision. If it can destroy trust and have an effect on the quality, suppliers, or the business as a whole, then again, don't do it.

(d) Do you have all the information you need to make a good decision? Get to the bottom of it. If you have any doubt about the truthfulness of an employee, client, or supplier, check the information.

(e) Is there mutual benefit? The big takeovers common in the late 1980s did not always benefit everyone and many employees were fired and companies were closed. Determine what the long-term results will be for all parties.

(f) How will it make you feel about yourself? Can you live with your decision? Will it erode your self-esteem? Will it make you feel proud? Let your conscience guide you.

(g) Was there adequate time? Was everyone concerned given enough time to plan, analyze past and current performance, and weigh pros and cons?

(c) Summary

Employees may come and go, but while they are employed by you, look upon them as partners in your business. You cannot demand their loyalty, but you can earn it. Make sure your employees are involved in composing your code of ethics, in monitoring it, and in revising it. Their participation is important to its initial and continued success. Assure that the code goes beyond the minimum expected by employees.

The Stadium Bakery in Calgary closes its doors for two weeks each summer to allow its small, but loyal, staff to all vacation at once. No one has to work harder to accommodate vacationing employees. The Fannie May Candy Shoppe encourages drivers with time on their hands during the slow summer months to set up their own businesses to augment their income, and it uses and promotes those new limo and moving services. The success of your business depends on the health, well-being, and attitude of your employees. Your code of ethics must reflect your commitment to them and they to you.

2. Your customers and clients

You don't have a business without someone who buys your product or service. Your code of ethics needs to state succinctly how you intend to do business with your customers — and that policy has to be made clear to everyone: employees, suppliers, competitors, and the customers themselves. (In another Self-Counsel book, *The Small Business Guide to Customer Relations*, my co-author, Brian Taylor, and I discuss the need to maintain good customer service and how to set up a workable program.)

Department stores like Woodwards of Canada and Rich's of Atlanta state simply that "the customer is always right." Even when a customer is blatantly dishonest, these stores operate on the premise that the majority are decent, honest people, and so they treat everyone equally. You may wish to spell out things more fully in your code of ethics:

- Who are our customers/clients?

- What will be our reception to them?

- What can they expect from us as individuals and as a business over the short and long term?

- How will we meet our competition?

Some customer/clients have very special needs. When Bill Daniels opened his Young Americans Bank in the Cherry Creek shopping district of Denver, Colorado in 1987, he had very specific customers in mind: children. In the first 6 months, he had signed up 3,000 — 6 times the number he had projected. His customers feel at home in a bank that has a T-shirt display, low counters, and, in particular, tellers who treat them with respect. Customers can borrow as little as $200 or finance their first car. They can attend seminars on using the bank and establishing good money skills.

If your customers have special needs, how you address those needs should be spelled out in your code.

3. Your suppliers

Of your three "senior partners," your suppliers are as important as your employees and customers, a fact many small business people often forget. When choosing supplies, you may not be able to attend to things as closely as Enrique does, choosing melons individually for his small kiosk in Granada, as described in chapter 1. But you do have to have suppliers you can count on. Here are some guidelines for choosing suppliers that you may wish to include in your code of ethics. Investigate the following areas:

- The reputation of the owner/manager and the reputation and experience of its staff
- The financial situation of the supplier
- The supplier's reputation with existing contractors
- The reputation of the supplier with employees
- The reputation of the supplier for meeting obligations, making deliveries, setting prices
- The condition of the plant (up to date, clean, safe?)
- The history of the company and its competition
- The reputation of its advertising and promotion (use the same guidelines as you would for your own; see chapter 5)

- The honesty and completeness of its parts books, sales manuals, brochures, price lists, and specification sheets

Selecting your suppliers needs to be done as carefully as choosing your employees. The suppliers must have a positive attitude toward you and your business. If your suppliers are greedy and unethical, if they look at doing business with you only as a way of making money at whatever cost, even if it means cheating you, providing you with inferior materials, or shortshipping orders, it will reflect on your business as a whole. A true partner wants you and your business to succeed and wants to be part of that success.

When choosing a supplier, ask yourself these questions, or, if you already have suppliers in place, use this as a checklist to review their performance:

- Has the supplier made a capital commitment to his or her business?

- Has the supplier made an honest commitment to me?

- Does the supplier deliver the specified supplies?

- Does the supplier deliver on time?

- Has the supplier the ability to look after product liability (insurance)?

- Does the supplier have reliable suppliers behind him or her? If the supplier manufactures a particular device for you but can't get a part from his or her own supplier, he or she won't be able to deliver to you.

- Does the supplier have the ability to do the job or are there always problems?

- Is the supplier competitively priced?

- Can or do we have rapport concerning problems?

- Does he or she advise well in advance if there is a problem? (The supplier who constantly puts you off with promises is not a good partner.)

- Does the supplier keep confidential information confidential? (While negotiating to be a vendor, a lot of business information is exchanged that should not become public knowledge.)

You should include guidelines for choosing and doing business with your suppliers in your code of ethics. But, remember, it is not all one way. Your relationship is a partnership and the behavior of the other partner, your business, must also be included. You don't want to be as dictatorial as Henry Ford who insisted his suppliers deliver parts in wooden crates which he then dismantled and turned into flooring for his Model Ts.

As a purchaser, consider including statements like the following in your code:

- We agree to the terms of the sale and adhere to that agreement.

- We live up to the terms of the contract concerning payment.

- We treat any knowledge gained about designs, specifications, drawings, or processes as confidential.

- We will not use knowledge gained to compete with suppliers.

- We will keep the suppliers apprised if we have problems that affect our relationship.

If you call for tenders, include the following statements:

- All tenders are confidential.

- All tenders will be treated fairly and equitably.

- All information will be shared equally.

- No information submitted will be shared with other vendors.

- All vendors will be given a fair chance.

This true, humorous, yet macabre, story about tenders illustrates the importance of writing this part of your business practice into your code. One rainy summer evening in a midwest U.S. city, I hailed a cab to take me to the airport. The driver was talkative and I asked why he used a station wagon for a cab.

"I've got three wagons. You see I used to have the contract with the coroner to take the stiffs to the morgue," he replied. I looked nervously into the back seat. "Yep, $40 a head," he went on, "some days we'd have as many as 20."

When I asked what happened to his business, he replied, "Oh, after five years someone at the coroner's office tipped off a bidder and he got the contract at $35. Now I've got three station wagon cabs."

Finally, your code of ethics should include directions to your employees regarding the "fine lines" of your relationship with your suppliers, which include the following issues:

- "Ethical" entertaining of suppliers by your business and vice versa. Business has been fraught with rumors regarding supplier-purchaser "entertainment" which has included prostitutes and holiday weekends. Keep entertaining to lunch only.

- A policy regarding gift giving and receiving, as mentioned earlier, needs to be clearly described.

- Who makes the decisions? You don't want any supplier working around you through your purchasing agent or a supplier who does an end run to you and ignores your purchasing agent.

Ethical behavior by both supplier and purchaser will make your "senior partnership" work. Your code of ethics will provide the blueprint for the behavior of you and your employees and the expected behavior of your suppliers. When putting together your code, you and your employees should consider every step you take in dealing with a supplier. Consider where ethics could be tested and make provisions for acceptable behavior and guidelines for decision making.

7

INTRODUCING AND MAINTAINING YOUR ETHICS PROGRAM

a. THE FINAL REVIEW

Once you have written your code of ethics, go over it again with a fine-tooth comb using the following questions to test its merit. These questions can also be used in periodic evaluations of the code.

(a) Does any item in the code affect or contradict another?

(b) Are the consequences of non-compliance clearly stated?

(c) Is our enforcement fair and just to all?

(d) Have we included practical guidelines for decision making?

(e) Have we created an environment for ethical behavior in our business?

(f) Are all our business systems — personnel, technical, financial — based on ethical practices?

(g) Have we allowed for open, ongoing communication at all levels?

(h) Does the code reflect a positive attitude to ethical business behavior as opposed to a judgmental attitude?

(i) Are we being fair? Are our policies, procedures, and ways of getting things done consistent or do they create conflict and inequities?

(j) Will our incentive systems really motivate? Will employees be rewarded for producing quality products and services?

(k) How will we handle situations where profit objectives are not met? Will ethics be set aside for profit?

(l) Are our short-term goals and long-term goals balanced and possible?

If you are satisfied that the answers to these questions are positive, then you can proceed to introduce your ethics program. The program must be good for you, your business, and your employees.

Michael Ovitz, president of Creative Artists Agency of Hollywood, puts time and effort into developing and taking care of his employees. His 65 agents are rewarded with large salaries and a share of the profits. In return, they approach their work with dedication, discipline, and fierce loyalty. As a result, the agency represents many of the top actors and directors in the business responsible for such movie blockbusters as *Rain Man* and *Mississippi Burning* and such television successes as "Golden Girls" and "Beauty and the Beast."

b. PUTTING YOUR CODE IN PLACE

Once you have a code of ethics approved by everyone involved, set up a meeting with your staff. In this meeting, present the code to everyone in a formal way. This will attach the importance to it that it deserves. Ask everyone to discuss the code. Be sure to go over methods of implementation, enforcement, and consequences of failure to comply. As well, use this time to discuss the training plan and the program evaluation system.

Give everyone a copy and indicate they are expected to refer to the code when making future business decisions. Give everyone time to read all the written material, then ask them to sign a card saying they have read the code and understand it. New employees and outside contractors or consultants should be asked to follow the same procedure.

c. DEVELOPING YOUR ETHICS TRAINING PROGRAM

Everyone involved must understand the code of ethics, its expectations, and how to deal with ethical problems and dilemmas. The best way to insure this is to implement a good training program. In any training program, communications should be encouraged and personnel should learn to think about ethics and to incorporate the code into their work activities.

Training should ensure that individuals explore, discuss, and define their values. Employees should develop a strong awareness of the company's values and must feel free to express their concerns without emotion or prejudice, knowing they will be given a fair, honest hearing. Training does not mean indoctrination; it should be an opportunity for two-way communication.

You can organize your training sessions in a variety of ways to suit the schedules of both your business and your employees. Everyone must be required to attend the sessions — no exceptions. Training sessions are for old and new staff.

1. In-house seminars

Perhaps the most convenient structure for your training session is an in-house seminar. Go over the mission statement and the code of ethics. Use examples of ethical problems that might arise and put forward a situation for discussion using the code as a measurement. (You can refer to the ethical problems posed in Appendix 2.) Break into small groups where each participant can outline an ethical situation for discussion. Emphasis should be placed on —

(a) safety,

(b) obedience to the law,

(c) honesty,

(d) reliability,

(e) respect for individual rights,

(f) concern for the environment, and

(g) fairness to all who have a stake in the final decision.

All of your staff should leave this type of seminar with a greater understanding of the ethical culture of the business and a feeling of pride in the company.

Seminar leaders can come from within the company or be hired from outside. Specialists, such as lawyers or accountants, might be brought in to speak on topics such as legal restrictions and government regulations.

2. Outside education

Employees may be sent to evening courses put on by educational institutions. If you don't send everyone, have those who do attend give in-house information sessions for the rest of the management and staff.

Often, such seminars are offered at professional or trade conventions or put on by reputable outside sources. For some resources, see Appendix 3.

3. Video training films

Some large companies produce their own videos that emphasize qualities they look for in their employees, such as integrity, tough-mindedness, team spirit, dedication, discipline, and loyalty.

While the videos maintain that work should be done within budget and on time, they also stress that quality comes first. You may be able to rent videos that pertain to your business.

d. ASSESSING YOUR TRAINING PROGRAM

Before spending a lot of your employees' time at a training session, make sure the plan you have designed has yes answers to the following questions:

(a) Does this program really train? Your program must have substance to make it worthwhile. Merely reading the credo and congratulating yourselves on putting it together will not get results. You must teach your staff to think about ethics and train them to deal with problems according to the company code.

(b) Does the program emphasize the positive? You want to motivate employees to feel proud about and adhere to the ethics program. Disciplinary deterrents, such as threats of pay loss or dismissal, are important, but the emphasis must be on the rewards of following the program.

(c) Is the program practical? Too often, training sessions are merely fun hours off work with no practical application to reality. If you hire outside consultants, be sure they have a good understanding of the ethical problems confronting your business.

(d) Does the program address ethical dilemmas? The program should address not just legalities and compliance, but also more difficult questions such as those concerning loyalty and fairness.

(e) Will the training insure that participants use the credo? You want everyone to have a clear understanding of the company they work for, be able to analyze ethical issues in their jobs, and apply the principles learned to their jobs. You want them to be able to make ethical decisions based on their training.

(f) Does the program have a follow-up component? Training should be ongoing and strongly supported and reinforced: not a one-shot effort.

(g) Is there a way to evaluate the effectiveness of the training? Short follow-up sessions presenting ethical dilemmas for group problem-solving are one method of measuring whether the training obtained the desired results.

e. A SUPPORT SYSTEM FOR YOUR ETHICS PROGRAM

You now have a mission statement, a code of ethics, and effective training, but you will not have a functioning ethics program until you have procedures to make it work. You must develop clear and simple systems to handle complaints, conduct impartial investigations, define standards of judgment, ensure fair hearings, and reach objective, responsible decisions.

An ethical program only becomes a part of the company's business practice when it is used. There must be a means in place to determine unethical behavior and report it knowing that there will be a fair hearing and objective decision making.

The following are suggested ways you can put in motion some of the systems you will need.

(a) Provide opportunities for open discussion on ethical issues, either hypothetical or actual.

(b) Provide guidance for yourself and employees when making a business decision. You might ask the following questions:

(i) Have I defined the problem accurately?

(ii) How would I define the problem if I were the other persons involved?

(iii) Do I have all the facts?

(iv) What are my options? Are they legal? Are they morally right? Are they beneficial? How did this situation occur in the first place?

(v) Will my decision regarding the problem injure anyone?

(vi) When I make my decision, could I defend it before those involved, my immediate boss, top management, my family, my friends?

(c) Appoint a special ethics committee to oversee the investigation of complaints. Committee members must have high personal integrity and demonstrate high business ethics.

(d) Have an ombudsman responsible only to you to review and report complaints. This person must be chosen with great care because of the power invested in the position.

(e) Determine the procedures you wish followed in cases of a complaint. Do you want complaints put in writing? If your business is big enough, do you wish to set up a telephone hotline so employees may anonymously report complaints?

(f) Evaluate the program at set periods. Keep records to audit the success of your procedures. Inform all management and employees of the results.

(g) Change the structure of your business to encourage ethical decision making. You may have to allow more decision making at the lower levels.

(h) Determine if and how your code will adapt to changing circumstances.

Your ethics policy is not cast in stone and should accurately reflect the company's way of doing business. At the same time, it should not be so flexible it can be twisted to cover any action or it will be useless.

f. REPORTING UNETHICAL BEHAVIOR

Part of your ethics program must be the procedures employees should follow when reporting unethical behavior, for example:

(a) Determine the nature of your complaint. Is the act you are reporting illegal? Does it represent non-compliance with the company's code of ethics?

(b) Get the facts straight and document them. Can you prove what you say? Were you present when the act in question occurred or is your information secondhand? Photocopy any pertinent papers and take them home for documentation.

(c) Use the best method to report the complaint. Discuss it with your supervisor, take it to the ethics committee or ombudsman, or use the hotline, whichever is the recommended procedure for your business.

g. ENFORCING THE CODE

To ensure compliance with the code you establish, you must have an enforcement system in place. As I stated previously, to accomplish this, you may appoint a committee or ombudsman, and you may wish to create a hotline for complaints and information. Let's look at these ideas more closely.

1. Ethics committee or ombudsman

Your code should include guidelines concerning who will serve on the committee, how long they will serve, and how many members will sit on the committee. Enforcement personnel should not all be management level and should have strong, demonstrated, ethical standards of behavior. How will the ombudsman be chosen? For how long? What is his or her area of jurisdiction? How is confidentiality assured?

The committee or ombudsman must know whom to report to and who will be responsible for seeing that decisions are carried out.

You must also decide and make clear in what form enforcement personnel will receive its information regarding unethical behavior. An appeal system should be set up as well so that those who come under the scrutiny of the committee have the opportunity to contest its decisions.

Confidentiality must be mandatory if you expect employees to respect the system. You will have to determine whether the role of ombudsman will be a full-time position or part of another job. The enforcement personnel should not be perceived as being on one side or another of the company structure or any issue in particular. They must set themselves apart and be able to act in a fair and honest manner.

2. Hotline

If you decide to run a telephone hotline, you will need to hire or assign people to answer the telephone or you could set up an answering machine. Telephone personnel should obtain from callers as much detail as possible, such as names, date, time, and place, concerning alleged infractions. They will also need to know what to do with the information they gather. Their responsibility to respect the anonymity of the callers should be impressed on them.

Once the information is in proper hands, whether that be a committee or an ombudsman, someone must follow through on the information. Finally, you should have some safety checks to follow so that no one will be falsely accused.

Once your ethics program is functioning, it must be ongoing and provide a constant foundation on which you conduct your business.

8
YOUR ETHICS PLANNING PROGRAM

This chapter is meant to help you develop your own ethics plan. Use the following material, which includes lists, questions, and worksheets, to customize a plan that will be effective for your company.

a. AGENDA FOR A BUSINESS ETHICS PROGRAM

Here is a suggested agenda for developing your ethics program. You might use the flowchart on page 87 to work out your timelines for each stage of development.

1. *Commitment and leadership by owner/managers*

2. *Involvement and commitment by employees*

3. *Structural changes to company:* The company may have to be restructured to encourage ethical decision making at all levels.

4. *Mission statement:* If the company does not have a mission statement, you must determine your purpose for being in business.

5. *Code of ethics:* Include guidelines for making ethical decisions, the means of reporting unethical behavior, and how enforcement will take place. The code must be in a form that can be used by all employees.

6. *Enforcement means in place:* Establish an ethics committee, ombudsman, hotline, or judiciary board.

7. *Communication of program:* The program must be introduced to all employees initially. Communication

must be ongoing. It must be publicly displayed, procedures for reporting unethical behavior must be reinforced, and all new employees must be educated.

8. *Training:* Management and employees should be trained in ethical decision making based on your company code of ethics. Training may be generated internally or led by outside trainees. New employees must be trained and employees who have problems in ethical decision making retrained.

9. *Commence program:* Set a definite date to begin the program. A strong commitment must be voiced by the owner/manager. It will be his or her example that will directly affect the success of the program.

10. *Evaluation of program:* Identify, monitor, measure, report, and evaluate the effect of the program. Keep records of numbers, not names of reports and questions. Results should be reported to all involved: managers, employees, and stockholders. Good news will motivate employees.

11. *Adjust and add:* Allow for a yearly review to evaluate, add, or adjust the code itself as well as the reporting and enforcement procedures.

12. *Reward and motivate:* Your business ethics program must not be perceived as tactics of spying or punishment. The ethics program must be positive: a source of strength and pride. Rewards should be all encompassing, a tribute to all employees for their loyalty, dedication, and ethical behavior.

13. *Consistency:* There must be consistency in the decision-making process and the enforcement of policy. Any approved deviation from the code will negate its purpose.

TIME LINE FOR ETHICS PROGRAM

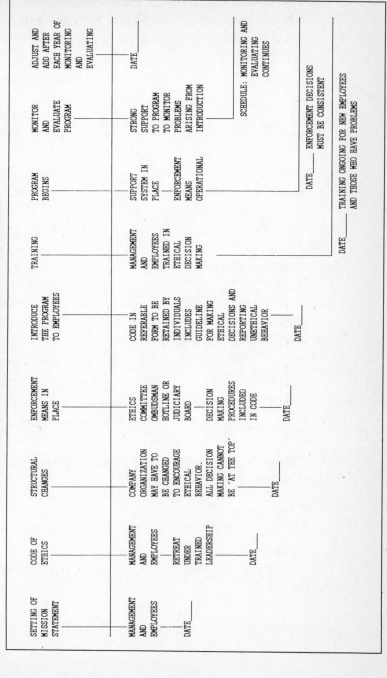

b. OWNER/MANAGEMENT CONSIDERATIONS BEFORE SETTING UP AN ETHICS PROGRAM

1. How accountable can we be?

2. How responsible can and should we be?

3. What resources can we provide?

4. How committed can we be?

5. What do we expect from this program?

c. WRITING THE MISSION STATEMENT AND CODE OF ETHICS

1. Who will be involved in writing our mission statement and our code of ethics?

2. Who will chair proceedings?

3. When will we meet?

4. Where will we meet?

5. What is our deadline for completion of mission statement and code of ethics?

6. Does anyone need release time/overtime in order to participate?

OUR MISSION STATEMENT: (Try to keep it to one sentence. It should be your purpose and objective for being in business.)

d. OUR CODE OF ETHICS

What do we need to say about:

1. Our product(s)

2. Our service(s)

3. Our employees

4. Our customers

5. Our suppliers

6. Safety

7. The environment

8. Our community

9. Shareholders

10. Others

e. A CHECKLIST FOR THE CODE

(If you answer any of the following questions NO, go back to the drawing board.)

1. Does any one feature of the code affect or contradict another?

❑ YES

❑ NO

2. Will there be any confusion if all these features are practiced at the same time?

❑ YES

❑ NO

3. Are the results for non-compliance clearly stated?

❑ YES

❑ NO

4. Is our enforcement fair and just to all?

❑ YES

❑ NO

5. Have we included strong guidelines for decision making?

❑ YES

❑ NO

6. Have we created an environment for ethical behavior in our business?

❑ YES

❑ NO

7. Are all our business systems — personnel, technical, financial — based on ethically based practices.

❑ YES

❑ NO

8. Have we allowed for open, ongoing communication at all levels?

❑ YES

❑ NO

9. Does the code reflect a positive attitude to ethical business behavior as opposed to a judgmental attitude?

❑ YES

❑ NO

f. TRAINING FOR MANAGEMENT AND EMPLOYEES

1. Why do we need an ethics training program?

2. What needs to be taught?

3. Who needs the training?

4. Who should teach it?

5. How can we assure training is being used?

6. How often do we need training?

7. How can we work ethics training into our ongoing business plans?

g. ENFORCING THE CODE

(You may have one or a combination of the following methods of enforcing your code. Whichever you decide on, answer these questions before you put it into action.)

1. Ethics committee or board

(a) Who will serve?

(b) How long will each member serve?

(c) How will a chairperson be appointed?

(d) To whom will the committee report?

(e) What form will the committee receive its information regarding unethical behavior?

(f) Who is responsible for seeing that the decisions of the committee are carried out?

(g) Does the code of ethics state clearly what is considered unethical behavior?

(h) What authority does the committee have if the code has been breached?

(i) What action will result in reprimand, fine, firing?

(j) How can the decision of the committee be appealed?

2. **Ombudsman**
(a) Is the role of ombudsman full time or in addition to other duties?

(b) What is the criteria for the position?

(c) Who will make the selection?

(d) How will confidentiality be maintained?

(e) How long is the appointment for?

(f) To whom will the ombudsman report?

(g) In what form does the ombudsman receive information regarding unethical behavior?

(h) How will the decisions of the ombudsman be carried out?

(i) How does the code of ethics provide the ombudsman with a clear measurement for making and enforcing decisions?

(j) How can the decision of the ombudsman be appealed?

3. Hotline

(a) Who will answer the hotline?

(b) Where does the information go?

(c) Who follows through on the information?

(d) Can the caller be assured of anonymity?

(e) How will confidentiality be maintained?

(f) How much detail concerning persons, date, time, place, must the caller provide?

(g) What are the safety checks to follow so that no one will be falsely accused?

h. MEASURING SUCCESS

You will know your ethics program is working when the following statements accurately describe the positive feelings of you and your staff toward your business.

- PURPOSE: The mission of our organization is communicated from the top. The owners/managers are committed to the ethics program. My own business behavior sets the example.

- PRIDE: We are proud of ourselves, our work, our company. We would not do anything to jeopardize our reputation or that of our fellow employees or our company.

- TIME: What we do today will ultimately affect us in the future. We do not look for short-term gain at the risk of long-term pain. We care not only about profit, but how we achieve profit. We take time to consider all aspects before making a decision.

- COMMITMENT: We not only believe in our purpose, we are committed to it. We make sure all our actions and decisions are in accordance with our commitment to our code.

- EVALUATION: We the owners, managers, and employees can take time to evaluate our program, discuss changes, set new goals and determine how we would reach them.

- COMMUNICATION: We know we have open communication between management and employees and between employees and employees. What is communicated is honest.

- FAIRNESS: We know that a deviation from the code of ethics will have a fair hearing and will be dealt with without prejudice or bias.

- TRUST: We have trust in the procedure and the people who make decisions concerning unethical behavior.

- LOYALTY: We have a strong sense of loyalty to our company for we know the company has made a commitment to us and considers us to be valuable assets.

APPENDIX 1
EXAMPLES OF CODES OF ETHICS

a. ROYAL BANK OF CANADA

The over 38,200 employees of the Royal Bank of Canada receive copies of *Code of Conduct: Principles of Ethical Behavior* at the time of their hiring. The code is reviewed during semi-annual performance appraisal reviews.

The overall purpose of the Royal Bank of Canada is to ensure survival as a progressive free enterprise and continuity through short- and long-term profitability so that it may fulfill its responsibilities in society.

These responsibilities are to —

- Provide potential and existing clients, throughout the world, with the broadest possible range and highest quality of banking and financial services

- Provide employees with opportunities for personal development and achievement and equitable compensation

- Provide investors with an attractive and continuing return on their capital

- Act as a responsible corporate citizen whose activities benefit the community, nation, and society.

To attain this purpose and to meet these responsibilities, the bank considers it must —

- Give good value — contributing rather than exploiting

- Deal with people and institutions fairly and honestly

- Recognize and respect each person's rights, individuality, and human dignity

- Be a responsible citizen
- Be a leader, unceasingly striving for excellence in everything they do.

b. J.C. PENNY CO.

One of the first codes of ethics was introduced by J.C. Penny Co. in 1928. It is clearly and simply written:

The Penny Idea

- To serve the public as nearly as we can to its complete satisfaction.

- To expect for the service we render a fair remuneration, and not all the profit the traffic will bear.

- To do all in our power to pack the customer's dollar full of value, quality, and satisfaction.

- To continue to train ourselves and our associates so that the service we give will be more intelligently performed.

- To improve constantly the human factor in our business.

- To reward the men and women in our organization through participation in what the business produces.

- To test our every policy, method, and act in this wise: "Does it square with what is right and just?"

c. THE BANFF CENTRE

The Banff Centre for Continuing Education publicly states it is a unique institution playing a special role in the advancement of Canadian cultural and professional life. Concentrating on intensive, residential training of a practical, non-degree nature, the School of Fine Arts, the School of Management, and Educational Conference Services all seek to meet national and international standards of excellence while continuing to serve the people of Alberta and beyond in areas of the arts, management studies, arts management, environmental studies, and educational conferences.

d. VOICE AND SPEECH TRAINERS ASSOCIATION (VASTA)

PURPOSES

1. To encourage the development and maintenance of optimal standards in the education and training of voice and speech teachers, coaches and consultants in theater, film, television, communication, and video arts.

2. To develop guidelines and establish training programs for individuals wishing to become such specialists.

3. To establish and provide criteria to individuals, theaters, conservatories and universities for evaluating the qualifications of these specialists.

4. To establish a code of ethics for the membership of this association.

5. To encourage voice trainers to explore approaches to training in such a way that actors' and all other professional speakers' voices will serve their emotional, communicative, and creative needs.

6. To encourage the safe and healthful use of the vocal instrument.

7. To promote the skills of the voice and speech specialists in such a manner that he or she is recognized as being integral to the teaching of acting for theater, film, and television and to the development of all professional voice users.

8. To promote recognition, credibility, and visibility for qualified voice and speech specialists and to en-

courage hiring, promoting, and granting of tenure to qualified and ethical individuals.

9. To encourage and facilitate ongoing education as well as exchanges of knowledge and information among professionals in the field.

CODE OF ETHICS

Every member of this organization must agree in writing to subscribe to the following code of ethics:

As a professional voice and speech, coach or consultant in theater, film, television, communication, and video arts adopting this code of ethics, I agree to —

1. Offer the best instruction of which I am capable.

2. Present accurately my training or expertise.

3. Give full credit to the work of colleagues.

4. Respect the rights of colleagues to advocate methodologies with which I may not agree.

5. Give my students objective and knowledgeable assessment of their work.

6. Refer a student when there is need to a physician, psychologist, speech pathologist, singing teacher, body alignment expert, voice and/or speech teacher or another appropriate specialist.

7. Maintain confidentiality regarding my students.

8. Honor a director's interpretation of a play, a film, or another production in rehearsal.

9. Discharge students whose stated goals have been achieved.

10. Pursue continued professional growth.

APPENDIX 2
ETHICAL DILEMMAS

This book has set out some guidelines and questions to use when confronted with an ethical question or dilemma. You can study the following cases yourself or use them as a basis for group discussion. Following all of the questions are comments on each.

a. THE DILEMMAS

1. A store clerk, Alice, works shift work in a women's wear boutique in a mall. Two other sales women work rotating shifts so that there are always two clerks in the store. The store manager works from 8:00 a.m. to 5:00 p.m. which leaves the evening shift to two clerks. Shoplifting is always a problem in a store that opens into a high-traffic mall. Over the past six months, the boutique has had high losses due to shoplifters. While working an evening shift, Alice observes the other clerk, Jean, take an expensive sweater from the display to the back of the store. When it comes time to close the store, Alice sees the sweater in the large purse that Jean always carries. What should she do?

2. The president of a small company that manufactures specialized mining equipment is in the process of hiring a sales manager. The president is delighted to find that one of the applicants is presently the sales manager of one of his strongest, most successful competitors. During the interview, the sales manager subtly lets the president know that if he is hired he can bring several of his present employer's large

accounts with him. He not-so-subtly indicates that he would expect a large under-the-table bonus for doing so. The president knows if he hires the sales manager his company would benefit greatly from the accounts and would increase company profits. What should he do?

3. The sales manager of a small company that manufactures ski clothing and equipment is interviewing prospective sales people. One of the prospects is presently working for a competitor. During the course of the interview, he lays a computer disk on the desk and indicates that it contains valuable information on all of his present employer's accounts and future designs. He also states that if he is hired the disk would remain on the sales manager's desk.

The sales manager excuses himself to relate the incident to the president who says, "The guy is a crook. We don't want him working for us. Tell him he's hired, put nothing in writing, keep the disk, and when he gets back to you, deny you hired him."

What should the sales manager do?

4. A small company has dealt with the same office supplier for many years. In the last two years, service has become sloppy and orders have arrived incomplete and, in some instances, damaged. The office manager has spoken to the supplier on several occasions with no results. When the contract runs out, she doesn't renew it but investigates using another supplier and finally decides on Company X. In setting up the contract, she gives them a copy of the company's

code of ethics and refers the salesperson to the section on ethics and suppliers. One of the issues dealt with is gifts: the company will neither receive nor give gifts to suppliers.

A week after the contract is signed, a gift is delivered to the office manager's home. The supplier has sent her an unusual antique music box. The supplier has obviously taken time to discover that the office manager collects antique music boxes and further time to search for one that is particularly valuable and unique.

The office manager faces an ethical dilemma. She covets the music box for it would add greatly to her collection, but to keep it would be against company policy. What should she do?

5. An untenured college lecturer is asked to speak in a distant city. It is quite a coup for him as it will give his research exposure to a large audience. He sees it as not only prestigious for himself, but also for the college. He speaks to his department head who has never supported his research. The head reluctantly gives approval.

The lecturer arranges and pays for another lecturer to take three of his classes while he is away. He selects the materials and approves the lesson plan for the replacement lecturer, announces his intent to his students, and leaves in high spirits.

Upon arrival in the city where he is to give his talk, he is interviewed by a national paper and local television station. His talk goes well.

Returning to the college, he finds he has been suspended from teaching and must meet with the college president to answer written charges from his department head that he left the college and his classes without informing the department head. What can the lecturer do?

6. Mary has spent many years recruiting and training the members of her department in a small resources company. Advancement within the company is limited because of the numbers and because of employee loyalty.

Mary hired John right out of university. In eight years with the company, he has proven to be a very capable employee. Mary has seen to it that John has had extra training financed by the company. John comes to talk to Mary about an offer he has had from another larger company that would allow for further advancement. He is not threatening to quit; he wants advice. What should Mary do?

7. You are going to set up and introduce an ethics program in your company. Rather than put someone from within the company in charge, you decide to hire from outside. One of the applicants has wide experience in the area of protocol and decorum including some years in service at the White House during the Nixon administration. His name is Jeb Stuart Magruder. Would you hire him?

8. You operate a small home construction company building homes in a city sub-division. In the past three months, you have suffered some major losses due to stealing. Lumber,

tools, hot water heaters, insulation, even bath tubs have been stolen. Your supervisors have carefully checked and locked homes and tool sheds at the end of each work day. You have also made the checks yourself, but in the morning, losses are reported. There is no sign of forced entry. You have your own security group headed by a long-time employee with whom you bowl each Thursday. You have begun to suspect the thefts are being committed by someone in security. What do you do?

b. THE ANSWERS

1. Stealing is against the law — number one in determining if an action is ethical or not. Before accusing Jean of stealing, Alice must find out if, in fact, she had bought the sweater. She can do so by checking employee purchase receipts. (Employees in the company receive a discount on all purchases and a record is kept of their purchases.) If she discovers that Jean did not buy the sweater, Alice must document what she saw: the date and time she observed the action and the style, color, and size of the sweater.

The ethical dilemma Alice faces is whether to confront Jean or go directly to the manager. If Alice believes Jean to be dishonest and responsible for stealing a number of items, she is dealing with someone who may not hesitate to "frame" her. Alice is not in a position to demand Jean change her behavior, so she would be better to report her findings to the manager.

2. If the president hires the sales manager, his company can reap short-term benefits: more profits. But in the long term, that decision is not fairly balanced. His company will benefit, but his competitor will lose accounts. The president will have

to balance these short-term profits against a reputation for "stealing" personnel and accounts. The president, by paying a "bonus" to the sales manager, is also giving the sales manager a strong example of the ethics of his company. If he hires the sales manager under these circumstances, he sets a precedent for further shady deals.

The president should turn the man down. His own personal ethics will help him determine whether he goes one step further and informs his competitor of the offer made by the sales manager.

3. If he wasn't aware of it before, the sales manager now realizes he is working for an unethical boss. The company may have a code of ethics but it is obviously not being supported or practiced by the president. The president's comment that the salesman is a crook is ironic for the president is asking his sales manager to lie and steal.

Since the sales manager has about five minutes to comply, he obviously doesn't have much time to change the personal ethics of his boss, but he can try. At least by doing so he is proving himself to be an ethical employee. He can point out the ramifications of complying with his boss' order. If the boss insists, the sales manager finds himself in an ethical dilemma. Unless he wishes to compromise, his only ethical action would be to refuse to do as asked, which could result in being fired, or he could quit.

4. There is only one answer. She returns the music box to the supplier. She also strongly, but pleasantly, reinforces the ethical terms of the company/supplier relationship. She asks the supplier to reread the book of company ethics regarding this relationship and lets it be known that living up to the contract by supplying good service and good products is what is expected. She keeps the call pleasant and positive, but

the supplier should be alerted so that the relationship can continue based on the ethical credo of the company.

If she wants the music box, she should see if the gift indicates in what store it was purchased. She shouldn't offer to buy it from the supplier because it would make the matter messy. She wants to keep it clean and complete the conversation as quickly as possible.

5. The lecturer is in a difficult position. The department head is not just unethical, but dishonest and probably jealous. The lecturer has no documentation to prove he had permission from the department head to be absent. Here is a situation where you should ask for permission in writing and get the reply documented.

The person who took over the professor's classes has only the word of the lecturer that he had been given permission to leave his classes. The documentation presented by the department head indicated his first knowledge that the lecturer was not on campus came from reading the article in the national newspaper. This example is based on an actual case. This is what actually happened:

The president placed a letter of reprimand in the lecturer's file and deducted pay for the classes he did not teach. The lecturer took his case to the college ethics committee and, because of lack of documentation on both sides, he was not reprimanded or fined, and the letter was removed from his file and destroyed. As an untenured lecturer, he realized he had a formidable enemy in the department head and little support from the president. He quit his position and became an independent consultant based on his research. In time, his work became widely recognized and he was honored by the college as a former lecturer! The department head found others to challenge and was finally chastised by the ethics committee for "blackmailing" his lecturers and lost his position. In the long run, the code of ethics of the college stood the test, but not without casualties.

6. Mary is faced with an ethical dilemma, not an ethical issue. An ethical issue can usually be solved by following the company's code of ethics. A dilemma is much more complicated and involves multiple values and the difference between "doing the right thing" and "wanting to do the right thing — but." On one hand, she would like to advise John to stay with the company. She knows he is a strong member of her department. Strong employees make managers and supervisors look good. She may have a difficult task finding another employee as good as John. Also, the company has invested in John at her recommendation. On the other hand, Mary has obviously inspired loyalty in herself and the company, which is why John is seeking her advice.

If Mary advises John not to take the job, she manages to hold on to a valued employee — for a while. If John finds he has nowhere to go in the company, he may become disheartened and bitter and not give the same effort to his job. If Mary advises John to go for the new job, she may have to find someone to take his place, but in the long run John may have a great influence on the company from the "outside." He will be a strong supporter in whatever position he achieves.

Mary should discuss the move carefully with John, looking at the pros and cons, and John should make up his own mind, with the encouragement and support of Mary.

7. This is not a facetious question. Jeb Stuart Magruder served several months in prison for his role in the Watergate cover-up. He was hired as the Chairman of the Columbus Ohio Commission on Values and Ethics. His actions would appear to be in direct contradiction to his appointment. You would do better to hire someone who has demonstrated

ethical behavior in his or her previous jobs and personal life. Employees need leaders who personify what they preach. Any doubt about how leaders would act when confronted with a right or wrong, legal or illegal, situation, places their leadership in question.

8. Stealing is illegal, so you can call in the police to investigate, but this is more of an ethical dilemma than a legal issue because your friendship is involved. Before going to the police, you need to put the problem before all of your employees. Explain the problem and say that if it doesn't stop, the police will be called in. Also explain that you intend to do an internal investigation even if it does stop because you won't tolerate such action.

Arrange to meet with your supervisor and the head of security to implement the internal investigation. Your security head could have become lax in doing his job. It may be a member of his group or a canny contractor who is doing the stealing. Don't accuse anyone until you have evidence. If the evidence clearly isolates your friend and he is guilty, have him charged and fired. Clean up from inside.

APPENDIX 3
WORKSHEET KEYS

WORKSHEET #1

The basics

If you answered (a), then you are obviously convinced that you own or manage a top company. If you are convinced yourself, you will have no problem convincing others, your employees and your clients.

If you answered (b), you are probably being positive but realistic. Before you start an active program in company ethics, take a good look at the positive attributes that have put your company into the top 50% while evaluating steps that would put it into the top 25%. You may find that the answer is related to having a strongly enforced code of ethics.

If you answered (c), you should be concerned about why you rated your company here. Does it have to do with sales and profit alone? Is it because you are not sold on the company's activities, the way you have been doing business, or the way you treat clients and employees? Before you implement an ethics program, take a long, hard look at why you rated your company in the bottom 50% when just one percentage point separates the top 50% from the bottom 50%. Remember, if you are not sold on your company, you won't be able to sell anyone else on it.

Ability

If you answered (a), you obviously have a lot of confidence and self-esteem. You must make sure that the confidence and self-esteem does not turn to arrogance and false pride. Arrogance and false pride can interfere with communication and balanced thinking, both of which are necessary if you wish to act in an ethical manner.

If you answered (b), you obviously have self-confidence and self-esteem, perhaps even some modesty. You may wish to set some goals for yourself to make that rating higher without jeopardizing any of your basic moral tenets. If you put yourself in the top 50%, it indicates a positive attitude, one that makes it natural for you to set goals for yourself and achieve the quality of self-esteem without arrogance which makes for a strong leader.

If (c) was your answer, you are obviously questioning your abilities, realize that you are in the wrong field, or have a negative attitude toward yourself and your capabilities. Before you take a leadership position in establishing a program of ethics for your company, you must give attention to your leadership qualities because it will be your enthusiasm, self-confidence, and belief in the project that will make or break it.

Fostering pride

Grade yourself as a builder of employee self-esteem. Give yourself three points for every (a) answer, two points for every (b) answer and one point for every (c) answer, with the exception of questions 11 and 12 for which the only answer is (a). Rate yourself as a top builder of self-esteem if you achieved between 30 and 36 points.

Building trust

Give yourself three points for every (a), but give yourself no points for (b) or (c) answers. You cannot be seen to be inconsistent or favoring one person over another when it comes to building trust. You cannot use your power or position to exonerate yourself from normal courtesies. Remember, you set the example for everyone in the company. If you scored between 54 and 60, you rank high in the area of trust.

Communications

The only answer for·questions 1 to 3 is (a). Remember, you communicate not only by what you say but how you say it. Communication also comes through the respect you show for yourself and those around you in the way you dress and in your general decorum. For questions 4 to 16, give yourself three points for each (a) answer, two points for each (b) answer, and one point for each (c) answer. Rate yourself as a strong communicator if you scored between 40 and 48 points.

Honesty

1. If your answer is yes, you are setting a poor example for all employees. Give praise where it is due, but be prepared to deal honestly with poor performance. Guide and encourage the employee to a better performance.

2. Your answer should be yes. A good solid performance-review system gives employees confidence in you and the company. They know their performance will be treated fairly and honestly.

3. Your answer should be yes. This is the only policy: be sure you adhere to it. If you deviate from it even once, you and the company will be perceived as being dishonest or at the least soft on your own commitment.

4. You should answer no. Be up front with employees. Many feel they are being sent on courses as a punishment.

If you feel an employee needs further training, discuss the reasons for it before he or she is sent. If not, the negative attitude will prevent him or her from getting anything out of the training.

5. Your answer should be no. To do so would be unfair and dishonest. Training should be just that. An evaluation of performance should be made after training has been put into practice and monitored.

6. Be careful with this one. If you do this, you are asking your supervisors to be dishonest and rate good employees low in order to be perceived as a tough supervisor. Negativity breeds negativity. If you are always looking for the negative, you will get employees who act negatively, selfishly, and dishonestly to please you.

7. If you do, that employee and all the others will view you as unfair and unjust. Not only that, but the customer will distrust you also. He or she would question how you would react in other situations.

8. Remember, results can be short lived, but your action will be remembered and emulated by your staff. Shortcuts may save money but result in an inferior product. Shortcuts can show a lack of concern for the long-term interest of employees or customers. Employees may get even by being dishonest themselves.

9. If you do, you may meet the specifications of the contract but you will damage your reputation.

10. If you do, you may find the cost very expensive in the long run. Employees who must only produce "the bottom line" may be doing so in dishonest ways that will come back to haunt you and destroy your reputation and that of your company.

11. A policy that is not enforced is useless. If it is to have any meaning, it must be enforced. Let one employee get away with dishonesty and you set the standard for the rest.

12. Let the supplier know where you stand on this issue and don't compromise. You can continue to do business, but monitor the situation. If there is any further evidence of impropriety, get a new supplier.

13. Business ethics begin with basic honesty in the smallest way. Cheating is a betrayal of the first premise of honesty — honesty about oneself.

WORKSHEET #2

Pride and ability

1. If you answered (a), you are obviously convinced that this is a top company to work for. When you believe you work for the best company, you have tremendous pride in that company and that pride will affect your own performance. Do not let that pride become arrogance, however.

If you answered (b) you are being positive but realistic. You still have great pride in your company, but you may see ways for it to become even better. As an ethical employee, you would employ ethical means to achieve that goal.

If you answered (c), you should be concerned about why you gave the lower rating. If it has anything to do with the way the company does its business, treats employees, customers, or suppliers, then you should sincerely question why you are working for it or would want to work for it.

2. If you answered (a), you obviously have a lot of confidence and self-esteem. Don't allow them to turn to arrogance and false pride. Keep the way open to learning, developing, and good communication.

If you answered (b), you have self-confidence and self-esteem, but have given yourself room to improve. That improvement can come through setting goals of growth for yourself that will not put your basic moral values in jeopardy. If you wish to improve your skills, you should work for a business that values quality employees and includes training and opportunities for advancement in its mandate.

If (c) was your answer, you are obviously questioning your abilities. You may be in the wrong field or have a negative attitude toward yourself or your capabilities. You may be frustrated in your work and unhappy with your position. You may react negatively toward your supervisor and other employees. This attitude could make you vulnerable to unethical practices. You need to talk over your situation with your supervisor or get career counselling.

Fostering self-esteem in others

If you answered (a) to questions 1 to 5, you are concerned about your own self-esteem and the pride of others. If you answered (b) to questions 1 to 4, you are only human! While (a) is the best answer to 5, you must be sincere and not patronizing. For questions 6 to 8, (a) is the only acceptable answer. In question 9, (a) is the most acceptable but (b) indicates you are trying while (c) is not acceptable for any of the questions.

As a builder of your own and others' pride and self-esteem, give yourself three points for every (a) answer and two points for every (b) answer. If you achieved from 23 to 27 points, you rank high as a builder of pride and self-esteem.

Trust

Give yourself three marks for (a) answers and one mark for (b) answers, with the exception of questions 5 and 13 for which (a) is the only answer.

Speak to your fellow employees to clarify whether what they are doing is unethical and whether they are aware of it before speaking to a superior. Your perceptions may be incorrect.

If you achieved 35 to 39 points, your employer, fellow employees, and all with whom you do business have good reason to trust you.

Communications

Give yourself three points for (a) answers for questions 1 through 10. Give yourself two points for (b) answers for questions 5 to 7. Give yourself three points for answering (b) to question 11. Question 12 should be answered (a) obviously. Give yourself three points.

Do not accept change without question. This is not a negative or disloyal attitude, just good common sense. If you achieved from 30 to 36 points, rank yourself high as an ethical communicator.

Honesty

1. If you said yes, you set a poor example for all other employees. You also add to the overhead to run the business. Add up every employee's pilfering and you can put the company out of business. Call it what you want, it is stealing.

2. Your answer should be yes. If your company has a good, solid performance review system, it will allow a fair assessment of your performance and encourage training or retraining in areas where your performance needs strengthening.

3. It doesn't hurt to make your stance known. Once made, you must stick to it and not deviate.

4. If you feel that you are being asked to do something dishonest, you need to sit down and discuss it with whomever issued the order. If you can suggest another means to increase profit without compromising, you will probably get a better hearing. If there is no deviation from the order and you feel it is dishonest, you are faced with an ethical dilemma and the only answer may be to quit your job.

5. It is easy to rationalize that everyone else does it, but it is dishonest. Usually the type of company that offers kickbacks

is operating on shaky business principles and there will come a time when they will call in their favors putting you in an even more untenable situation.

6. This is a tricky question. There are many stories from big business that show that the person who blows the whistle ends up not only jobless but also blamed. Donna Hall reported financial misconduct of her boss, Jack Kempf, Minister of Forests in British Columbia, to the Attorney General. Kempf fired Hall before he was forced to resign his position and his membership in the Social Credit Party. (It didn't prevent him from being re-elected as an independent member of the legislature however!) Hall was eventually rehired in a new government position.

If you are sure you are working for an ethical company, but your boss is out of step, then make your report.

WORKSHEET #3

1. If you chose (a), it shows people look to you for leadership. If you chose (b), you come first, which does not make for being a team leader.

2. If you chose (a), you are a strong leader. If you, as the leader, tolerate any dishonesty, you create an environment for it to thrive. If you chose (b), you may be vulnerable on occasions to make dishonest behavioral choices yourself.

3. By choosing (a), you have indicated the leadership quality of being able to listen to others and come to a consensus. Be careful that you do not rely too heavily on others; bring your own strengths and commitment to the discussion. By choosing (b), you indicate you like running your own show. Your dogmatic approach could result in a high percentage of staff turnover, however. If your only goal is profit, you may sacrifice quality, staff honesty, and customer loyalty.

4. If you chose (a), it displays an inner drive to be part of a team, even to be a team leader. The number of captains of

industry, presidents, premiers, and prime ministers who were high school or university quarterbacks or team captains, is evidence that this choice is predominant among known leaders. The (b) choice may also indicate a leadership drive to "be the best." You may find this drive can be detrimental if you compete with members of your staff or find a need to display one-upmanship.

5. The (a) choice indicates a good human relations trait, but as a leader, if you have a serious doubt that is substantiated by fact, you must take action. If you selected (b) you have strong, aggressive leadership skills, but you must caution yourself not to take action until you have all the evidence and that you listen carefully before reacting. Do not provoke confrontation just because you enjoy it.

6. The (a) choice is a good choice for a leader. But if the solution is elusive, and you are spending too much time trying to find it, put your team to work on it or call on outside experts. The (b) choice is a dangerous one because if a problem is not solved, it will continue. Take the same advice as for (a) choice.

7. The (a) choice is the choice of a leader. A good leader motivates, nurtures, and inspires employees. The (b) choice is not the best choice for a leader. You may find yourself in competition with your employees. You also may not understand why others don't do as well as you do and may find it difficult to encourage them.

8. The interpretation is the same as for question 7.

9. The (a) choice is a good one for a leader, but you must be careful not to let personal friendship or emotions get in the way of good business judgment. You must not be overly patient or too soft if an employee's performance is wanting. The (b) choice is also partially good for a leader who must be responsible for "the bottom line." But making a profit should

not mean sacrificing employees. The successful leader rates employee well-being as a high priority.

10. Being willing to take the advice of others and not let your own ambition get in the way is very important for those in leadership positions. Investigations following the explosion of the Challenger space shuttle in 1986 showed that NASA managers ignored the advice of engineers to abort the launch because of the risk presented by faulty O-rings. Their own personal ambition caused the loss of seven lives and set the space program back several years.

APPENDIX 4
FURTHER RESOURCES

a. BOOKS

Berenbeim, E. *Corporate Ethics.* New York: The Conference Board Inc., 1987.

Iacocca, Lee. *Talking Straight.* New York: Bantam Books, 1988.

Olive, David. *Just Rewards — The Case for Ethical Reform in Business.* Toronto: Key Porter Books, 1987.

Pastin, Mark. *The Hard Problems of Management: Gaining the Ethics Edge.* San Francisco: Jossey-Bass, 1986.

Peal, Norman Vincent and Dr. Ken Blanchard. *The Power of Ethical Management.* New York: Morrow, 1988.

Solkin, Donald. *A Survey of Whistleblowers: Their Stressors and Coping Strategies.*

Toffler, Barbara Ley. *Tough Choices, Managers Talk Ethics.* New York: Wyley, 1986

b. MAGAZINES

Business Ethics
217 Division Street
Box 3473
Madison, Wisconsin 53704

Business and Professional Ethics Journal
University of Florida
Center for Applied Philosophy
240 ASB
Gainesville, Florida   32611

Journal of Business Ethics
Kluwer Academic Publishers
Spuiboulevard 50
P.O. Box 1700, 3300 AA
Dordrecht, Netherlands

U.S. Address:
101 Phillip Drive
Norwell, Massachusetts   02061

c. WORKSHOPS AND SEMINARS

Write to the following centers for information on their workshops and seminars on ethics and related topics. You should also check universities and colleges near you for classes, seminars, and workshops.

1. United States

Ethics Resource Center
1025 Connecticut Avenue N.W.
Suite 1003
Washington, D.C. 20036
(202) 223-3411

Trinity Center for Ethics and Corporate Policy
74 Trinity Place
New York, New York 10006
(212) 602-0816

Council on Economic Priorities
30 Irving Place
New York, New York 10003
(212) 420-1133

Lincoln Center for Ethics
Arizona State University — BAC 543
Tempe, Arizona 85287
(602) 965-2895

The Southwest Performance Group
7579 East Main Street
Suite 700
Scottsdale, Arizona 85251
(602) 941-8829

The Center for Business Ethics
Bentley College
Walthan, Massachusetts 02254
(617) 891-2981

2. Canada

Canadian Clearinghouse for Consumer and Corporate Ethics
Box 165, Postal Station S
Toronto, Ontario
M5M 4L7
(416) 783-6776

Canadian Network for Ethical Investment
Box 1615
Victoria, British Columbia
V8W 2X7
(604) 381-5942

d. OTHER HELP

If you decide to "blow the whistle," here are two groups you
or your lawyer can call:

Trial Lawyers for Public Justice
2000 P Street N.W.
Suite 611
Washington, D.C. 20036
(202) 463-8600

The Government Accountability Project
1555 Connecticut Avenue N.W.
Suite 202
Washington, D.C. 20036
(202) 232-8550

THREE OTHER TITLES BY
JACQUELINE DUNCKEL

THE BUSINESS GUIDE TO PROFITABLE CUSTOMER RELATIONS
Today's techniques for success

You need good service to attract customers and keep them coming back, and this book provides plans and programs that have been proven successful by other businesses. No matter what kind of business you are in, this book will help increase profits through improved customer relations. $7.95

Contents include:

- Customer service — what it is and what it is not

- The "why" of customer relations

- The value of service

- Developing a profitable customer relations program

- Setting goals for your business

- Putting your plan together

- Communicating your customer relations program to your employees

- Training employees

- Bringing it all together

THE BUSINESS GUIDE TO EFFECTIVE SPEAKING
Making presentations, using audio-visuals, and dealing with the media

Give dynamic speeches, presentations, and media interviews. When you are called upon to speak in front of your business colleagues, or asked to represent your company in front of the media, do you communicate your thoughts effectively? Or do you become tongue-tied, nervous, and worry about misrepresenting yourself and your business?

Effective communication has always been the key to business success, and this book provides a straightforward approach to developing techniques to improve your on-the-job speaking skills. This book is as easy to pick up and use as a quick reference for a specific problem as it is to read from cover to cover. Whether you want to know how to deal with the media, when to use visual aids in a presentation, or how to prepare for chairing a meeting, this book will answer your questions and help you regain your confidence. $7.95

Contents include:

- Preparing your presentation

- When and where will you speak?

- Let's look at visual aids

- Let's hear what you have to say: rehearsing

- How do you sound?

- What is your body saying about you?

- Confidence and self-control

- Packaging the presenter

BUSINESS ETIQUETTE TODAY
A guide to corporate success

Mind your manners and get ahead! Knowing when to open the door for a colleague or how to accept a gift can sometimes mean the difference between being pigeon-holed in your current position or being offered that attractive promotion. But times have also changed, and the rules once relied on are not always appropriate today. With the growing number of women in company boardrooms and the move toward more international business, a new style of behavior is often called for.

This book is as easy to pick up and use as a quick reference before that special event as it is to read cover to cover. $7.95

Contents include:

- To begin at the beginning — the etiquette of employment

- Department decorum

- Telephone manners

- Meeting manners and boardroom behavior

- Introductions and conversation

- Cultural courtesy

- Table manners

- Eating in and dining out

- Giving and receiving — the etiquette of business gifts

- Put it in writing

- Manners on the road

DISCARDED

ORDERING INFORMATION

All prices are subject to change without notice. Books are available in book, department, and stationery stores, or use this order form. (Please print)

IN CANADA
Please send your order to the nearest location:
Self-Counsel Press, 1481 Charlotte Road,
North Vancouver, B. C. V7J 1H1

Self-Counsel Press, 2399 Cawthra Road, Unit 25
Mississauga, Ontario L5A 2W9

IN THE U.S.A.
Please send your order to:
Self-Counsel Press Inc., 1704 N. State Street
Bellingham, WA 98225

Name _____

Address _____

_____

Charge to:
❑Visa   ❑ MasterCard

Account Number _____

Validation Date_____

Expiry Date _____

Signature _____

❑Check here for a free catalogue.

Please add $2.50 for postage & handling.
WA residents please add 7.8% sales tax

YES, please send me

_____copies of **The Business Guide to Profitable Customer Relations**, $7.95

_____copies of **The Business Guide to Effective Speaking**, $7.95

_____copies of **Business Etiquette Today**, $7.95